THE C

SCOTTISH HIGHLAND ROADS

The author and publisher have made every effort to ensure that the information in this publication is accurate, and accept no responsibility whatsoever for any loss, injury or inconvenience experienced by any person or persons whilst using this book.

Once again, Gillian is to be thanked for driving duties, this time on many forays into the countryside of Highland Scotland. Lauren gained herself many inheritance point credits by spending many hours processing the climb data. All photographs were taken by the author. Grateful thanks are extended to the following members of the Scottish cycling community for providing information and helpful advice: Peter Alexander (City of Inverness CC), John Bremner (Angus Bike Chain), Graham Doig (Moray Firth CC), Grant Ferguson (Boardman Elite), Paul Gareze (LRCC), Gordon Dick (LRCC), Lindsay Gillies (BBC Scotland), Janette Hazlett (Scottish Cycling), Grahame Hay (Perth United CC), George Hughes, Hamish Irvine (Cairngorm CC), Steven Liddle (Hebridean CC), Sandy Lindsay (Deeside Thistle CC), Hazel Manson (Mid Argyll Triathlon and CC), David Martin (Dundee Thistle RC), Chris Oliver (CTC Scotland), Laura Nicolson (Moray Firth CC), Brian Palmer (www.thewashingmachinepost.net), Owen Philipson (www.owenphilipson.com), Colin Smith (Shetland Wheelers) and Johnny Whiteside.

published by
pocket mountains ltd
Jenny Wren, Holm Street, Moffat DG10 9EB
www.pocketmountains.com

ISBN: 978-1-907025-26-6

Text copyright © John H McKendrick 2014
Photography copyright © John H McKendrick

The right of John H McKendrick to be identified as the Author of this work has been asserted by him in accordance with the Copyright, Designs and Patents Act 1988

A catalogue record for this book is available from the British Library

All route maps are based on 1945 Popular Edition Ordnance Survey material and revised from field surveys by Pocket Mountains Ltd, 2014. © Pocket Mountains Ltd 2014.

Printed in Poland

INTRODUCTION

There is historical precedent in Highland Scotland for using roads to inflict pain on people, and this guide taps into that legacy. In the aftermath of the 1715 Jacobite Rebellion, a network of military roads was commissioned by the British government to enable their troops to cross the length and breadth of the Highlands at speed to quell unrest and control unruly Jacobite sympathisers. Under the direction of General Wade (1724-1732) and General Caulfeild (1732-1767), 1100 miles of roads were constructed in less than fifty years. Inevitably, almost as quickly as they covered the miles in distance, these roads racked up the metres in altitude as they clambered their way to the lowest point or easiest route over the bealachs (passes or cols) connecting the glens that dissect the mountains of Scotland.

Time has not taken its toll on these roads nearly as much as one might expect. Investment and technological innovation have improved the quality and extent of the network beyond recognition, and it has become a community lifeline, vital for economic development.

Users of **The Cyclist's Guide to Hillclimbs on Scottish Lowland Roads** will already be familiar with The Rest and Be Thankful, an iconic climb which makes use of one of Caulfeild's military roads. Constructed between 1743 and 1749, the 1745 Jacobite Rebellion provided some unplanned disruption to the building schedule. Many more historic military roads appear in the selection of road hillclimbs featured in this second volume. Thankfully, it is now metalled surfaces that lie beneath the tyres of cyclists faced with the challenges of Bealach Ratagan, Carn an t-Suidhe, the Lecht and Loch na Craige.

Competitive hillclimb cycling on Scotland's roads

Every autumn, the modern-day equivalents of the Hanoverian forces – the regional cycling associations of Aberdeen & District, Dundee & District, and North of Scotland, and the many local cycling clubs – conspire to inflict pain on their members using the roads of Highland Scotland.

Road hillclimb racing is well-established throughout Scotland, with a national championship having been held every year from 1946 onwards. Since David Maxwell of Gilbertfield Wheelers won that inaugural competition, many great road cyclists have graced the podium, including Robert Millar (1977), Sandy Gilchrist (1970-76, 1978-81, 1983) and Jason MacIntyre (2000, 2006, 2007). However, despite the elevated profile and international reputation of so many of Highland Scotland's roads, few are used as national championship climbs; Lowland climbs such as Bonnyton Moor, Purin Den and Stow Hill tend to be the favoured venues.

This is not to suggest that road racing is neglecting what Highland Scotland has to offer. Dedicated hillclimb races are held across the Highlands, although these are often confined to club members. The cyclosportives that have become popular in recent years have brought climbers to embrace the challenges of Bealach na Ba (Bealach Mor and Beag), Cairngorm Ski Road (Cairngorm Classics), Cairn o' Mount (Snow Roads Sportive and Cairn o' Mount Challenge), Caterthun (Cairn o' Mount Challenge), Rannoch Moor and Glencoe (Buachaille Sportive), the Lecht (GTM King of the Mountains Sportive), Loch na Craige (Highland Perthshire Challenge) and Quinag (Ullapool Mor Sportive).

There are a number of longer races incorporating significant hillclimbs, such as the ascent of Dundee Law, used as a prologue to Dundee Thistle's two-day stage race, and duathlons are not averse to hillclimb challenges either – one example is the Loch Ness Duathlon which begins with an ascent of Carn an t-Suidhe.

Of course, hillclimbing is not just about rushing to the top, sweat bucketing and muscles screaming in pain. There is much to be said for slipping into the granny gear and effortlessly spinning your way to the crest of a hill while enjoying the scenery. Many cycle tourers and CTC club members share this outlook and may already be familiar with the road climbs that lie on Scotland's long-distance cycle routes. Most notably, Berriedale Braes are a real test for cycle tourers – whether met at the start or the end of an expedition between Land's End and John O'Groats.

This volume, showcasing 40 of the best climbs in Highland Scotland, is not just for the dedicated hillclimber, but is designed to encourage touring, competitive and casual cyclists to take on and conquer more of Highland Scotland's fantastically varied hillclimb challenges.

Climb like a mountain goat

If you have already experienced the pleasure and pain of road hillclimbing, you'll know that it is a skill that can be developed with practice. What follows is some advice for cyclists of all abilities – helping you enjoy the climbs more by spending less time on them!

10 elementary tips for climbing

- Know the hill and plan the ascent in advance
- Maintain momentum on approach to the climb, while avoiding the inclination to speed up. Speeding up on approach is more likely to result in burn-out than a quicker ascent
- Know your gears, and how and when to use them effectively. When climbing, you will be using lower than normal gears
- Gradually shift gears downwards on the ascent
- Anticipate shifting gear, and change before you have to. Shift down when you feel that your pedals are not spinning freely
- Keep upright in your saddle – in direct contrast to the flats (and the descents), more power is available on the climb when you are in an upright position

- Stand when you need extra power that cannot be met by shifting down gears (remembering that cycling out of the saddle burns more energy and should, therefore, be used selectively)
- Never get too tired or too hungry on the ascent – refuel and replenish depleted energy levels
- If the climb is too taxing to be completed without stopping, aim to stop where you are afforded some shade and shelter (under trees, buildings, etc)
- Invest in toe-clips (or preferably clip-in pedals) as this allows you to concentrate on pulling-up in your pedal rotations – this is the most efficient way to cycle, as gravity takes care of the downstroke.

10 tips to refine good climbing practice
- Try to keep your shoulders back (open) as this will improve oxygen intake
- A wider grip on the handlebars will help reduce breathing restriction (also making it easier to keep your shoulders open)
- Using lower gears with a greater number of pedal repetitions per minute (higher cadence) will place less strain on your knees than using higher gears with a lower number of pedal repetitions per minute (lower cadence). Aim for around 70 to 80 repetitions per minute for greatest efficiency
- Stand up momentarily on less taxing parts of the climb to use different muscle groups and to stretch your back. This is particularly important on longer climbs

- Only come out of the saddle in the steepest sections if you are sure that you will be able to stay out of the saddle until the gradient eases
- Only come out of the saddle when you are in the right gear for that part of the climb – it is difficult to shift gears when standing
- Get ready to come out of the saddle when one leg is at the top of the pedal stroke – as you push down on the pedal, pull yourself out of the saddle
- Look ahead and keep elbows slightly bent when out of the saddle to maintain good posture and strong breathing
- Practise – through time, knowing when to shift gear, when to come out of the saddle and when to push hard will become second nature. In particular, practise standing techniques on flats or shallow slopes
- Develop your strength – on the hill, or in the gym. Upper body strength and a strong core should not be overlooked – climbing needs more than strong legs.

10 final tips towards perfecting hillclimbing technique
- Lose weight! Climbing is a power-to weight-activity – world-class climbers tend to be slightly built. Of course, there are exceptions (Miguel Indurain immediately springs to mind). The basic rule is that the lighter cyclist does not need to generate as much power as the heavier cyclist as he or she has less

weight to carry uphill. Weight loss can also take the form of reducing bike weight. This might be a more palatable solution to maximising performance – do you really need that third water bottle?

- The main focus should be on improving climbing technique, rather than developing power through punishing hill repetitions
- For extra power without standing or changing down gears, pull on the handlebars, as this allows you to follow on by pushing harder on the pedals
- When standing, push your knees forward towards the handlebars, as this will help you gain extra power on your upstroke
- Try and shift up gears the moment before you stand and shift down gears when you return to a sitting position – this will help you to maintain a steady momentum
- Ride straight on all but the most severe inclines, as momentum, speed and energy will be lost weaving up the road
- Have some really low gears on your bike to assist with longer and steeper climbs
- Develop a regular pattern of breathing for greatest efficiency; for example by co-ordinating your breathing with your pedal strokes
- Visualise the climb and anticipate reaching the top at your planned speed
- Divide the climb into distinct sections and coax yourself through each section, focusing on the immediate challenge (while leaving aside enough energy to complete the whole climb).

Descend like a rolling stone

What goes up must come down, and though descents are not described in this guide, working through the route instructions in reverse offers some advance warning of what lies ahead. There are two challenges to meet in descent – fighting the wind and overcoming fear of speed.

10 top tips to get you started

- As for ascending, know the hill and plan the descent in advance
- Ensure that your bike is in good condition – in particular, that both brakes are in good working order
- Before descending, add layers at the summit to protect yourself from the wind-chill that your descent will generate
- Brake gently and gradually, as required
- Be aware that braking distances are greater when the road is wet
- Brakes on a bike are not as good as those on a car, so don't get too close to the vehicle in front of you on the descent
- Keep alert – constantly look ahead for gravel and potholes
- Always be prepared to stop if going around a blind bend
- Resist the urge to put your foot out for stability – it is more likely to throw you off balance and lead to a crash
- Descend within your comfort zone – an anxious mind is not well-placed to respond to unforeseen dangers ahead.

10 tips to take you down faster

- Think positive. Remind yourself that you are in control. Do not focus on hazards but how you will manage each hazard
- Where the profile of the descent allows, accelerate to a high speed at the start of the descent
- On reaching near maximum speed, tuck in and let gravity do its work
- Pedal, periodically, on longer downhills to prevent the build-up of lactic acid in your leg muscles and to maintain maximum speed
- Move your weight towards the back of your saddle. Bend elbows and knees, and relax, to absorb vibrations caused by rough surfaces
- Look as far ahead as possible to make timely adjustments in advance
- In going around tight bends, drive down your outside leg, lean on your inside leg (perhaps throwing the knee out) and lean your bike into the corner, while keeping the body slightly more upright
- Around tight bends, brake slightly on approach to (i) give you better traction and (ii) enable you to respond quickly if you need to brake more sharply to negotiate unforeseen hazards that may lie around the bend
- In cycling through rough areas of sand, gravel, dirt or uneven surface, try to brake in advance. On reaching an area of poor traction, keep a firm grip on the handlebars, place your feet at a position of equal height and do not further engage the brakes
- Where traffic allows, use apexing to straighten out corners – set up your line from the outside of the road well in advance of the corner, aiming to take the corner at the apex (mid-point) of the road, finally returning to the outside of the road when it straightens up after the bend.

Using this guide

The hills in this volume have not been selected because they rank as the 40 toughest climbs in Highland Scotland, although the vast majority would make it on to such a list. Nor is the compilation limited to the short sharp ascents that are the mainstay of the road hillclimb race circuit in Scotland. Rather, it aims to introduce the cyclist to the diversity of all that Highland Scotland has to offer. There are concave climbs that get progressively more difficult towards the summit (Wideford Hill above Kirkwall in the Orkney Isles) and convex climbs from which the cyclist spends the latter part recovering from the initial exertion on the steepest pitch (A'Chrois from Kenmore); short sharp bursts along steep escarpments (Achtuie at Drumnadrochit) and long drawn-out inclines (up to Rannoch Moor from the bottom of Glen Coe); busy urban roads (Dundee Law), rural roads frequented by tourists (the climb to the ski resorts at Cairn Gorm and the Lecht) and quiet country roads (the eerily silent climb up to Saxa Vord from the old military base at Valsgarth at the north end of Unst in the Shetland Isles); well-known roads (Calum's Road on the Isle of Raasay) and roads off the beaten track (the climb away from Reinigeadal on the Isle of Harris); and roads rising up from the coast (Hill of Findon above Gardenstown) and roads topping out at mountain summits (Craigowl Hill, near Forfar).

Two climbs are worthy of particular note,

each set against a spectacular landscape. One is a coastal climb, the other a mountain climb, widely revered as the toughest in Britain. Whether it is the brutality of a short blast away from the Mull of Kintyre lighthouse or the enduring pain of the 2000ft grind up Bealach na Ba that you find most challenging, there is no doubt that these will top the list of the most memorable in the Highlands.

Spanning the length and breadth of Highland Scotland, the routes in this volume are organised by region – Around Dundee, Angus & Perth; Aberdeen to the Grampians; Around Inverness; Sutherland, Orkney & Shetland; Northwest Scotland; The Hebrides; South of Fort William; Argyll; and Pitlochry & Western Perthshire. Included are remote mainland outposts such as Badrallach and the Mull of Kintyre, and six island climbs, as well as a range of hills within easy reach of the large towns and cities of Perth, Aberdeen, Dundee and Inverness.

The introduction to each region gives an overview of the road hillclimbing opportunities in the area and a summary of the featured climbs.

Each route starts with a brief overview of the climb, plus the length, total ascent, elevation range, average gradient, map references for the start point and end point, and the relevant OS Landranger map sheet. The route notes include key landmarks and hazards that need to be negotiated along the way and definitive start and end points.

A 'killer climb' (or most challenging section) has been identified for each route, while a contoured sketch map shows the route and its key features. The climb is also summarised by an elevation profile, the dimensions of which have been standardised. At the end of this guide, you'll find a statistics page listing the climbs in rank order by gradient.

The sheer size of Highland Scotland and the remoteness of some areas means that at some point the cyclist will have to make use of ferry, public transport or, in many cases, car to access some climbs. Details of the nearest railway station or ferry terminal are provided for each route.

The decision on how you approach each climb is left to you. If you are looking at each as a self-contained challenge to be tackled independently, you'll find everything you need in this volume. If you prefer to include some hillclimbs as part of a longer day out, the guidebooks in Pocket Mountains' **Bike Scotland** series make a particularly useful companion to many of these routes.

Final words

There is a healthy debate among the cycling community on the value and necessity of wearing a helmet. If you are undecided, then consider that a helmet won't diminish the thrills of hillclimbing and it may even help you focus less on the danger of descending. Protect that precious cargo with a well-fitted helmet!

11

With such easy access to the Grampian mountains, road hillclimbers could be forgiven for valuing the low-lying lands of Angus for their relative location rather than their inherent charm. What a mistake! This gateway to Highland Scotland has tons to occupy the hillclimber right on its doorstep – from city ascents in Perth and Dundee to the low-lying but abrupt rises of the Braes of the Carse, roads that top out in the higher hills of Sidlaw, and relentlessly drawn-out climbs up the glens that penetrate the southern edge of the Grampians. The accessibility of the routes between Perth and Dundee, in particular, has made them a firm favourite with hillclimbers, especially in the autumn season of competitive racing.

Featured in this chapter is the steep ascent known locally as Kilspindie (after the settlement it departs from) to reach

the highest point of the road under Pole Hill. Craigowl Hill, meanwhile, dominates the region, the radio transmitter on its summit accounting for its landmark status and road access to the top. Further afield is the long, drawn-out battle to gain the road just beneath the Caterthun hill forts from the southeast; the northwestern side (not featured in this chapter) makes for a shorter and stiffer alternative ascent.

There is no local climb to match that of Dundee Law in 'the City of Discovery', however. There are several routes up, but the route described here – embracing the wall of tarmac that is so aptly (or perhaps, you'll decide when you've completed it, inadequately) named Hilltown – is the most sadistic by far.

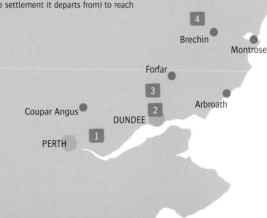

12

DUNDEE, ANGUS AND PERTH

13

POLE HILL KILSPINDIE, EAST OF PERTH

Distance 2.4 miles/3.8km
Total Height Gain 728ft/222m
Altitude Range 66-784ft/20-239m
Average Gradient 5.8%
Start Road bend (NO 221257)
End Parking place (NO 197266)
Map OS Landranger 53
Rail Perth Station (7 miles)

The highest point of road over the Braes of the Carse is reached on its longest, most gruelling hillclimb. Be prepared for some stiff ramps which intensify the severity of the early ascent.

It's a steady climb away from Kilspindie, which lies on the flat plain of the Carse of Gowrie at the foot of the steep bank of the Braes of Gowrie. At the end of the initial straight, follow the switchback to the right, signed for the church and Dalreichmoor. The road narrows around the turn and bends right, giving a steady climb which eases up as it veers left away from a passing place.

A sharp 90° left turn at Kilspindie Manse marks the start of a long steep stage, where the gradient picks up after passing the fork to the right. For much of this section, the road is hemmed in by a grass bank on the left and trees to the right, though you have good forward vision on the straights. Gentle bends and open views over the valley follow as the trees thin out.

After a switchback over the Evelick Burn to the right, the climb stiffens as the road clambers up the spur on the north side of the valley. A sweeping bend to the left carries the road over the spur, with the gradient easing as it straightens to aim directly for Balmyre Farm, though it picks up again slightly beyond the semi-detached

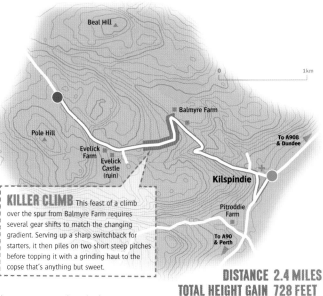

KILLER CLIMB This feast of a climb over the spur from Balmyre Farm requires several gear shifts to match the changing gradient. Serving up a sharp switchback for starters, it then piles on two short steep pitches before topping it with a grinding haul to the copse that's anything but sweet.

DISTANCE 2.4 MILES
TOTAL HEIGHT GAIN 728 FEET
AVERAGE GRADIENT 5.8%
CLIMB PROFILE

houses on approach to the farm.

The third and final switchback, reorienting you left away from the farm, signals the start of the toughest stretch so far. Initially steep at the turn, it briefly levels off, then stiffens as it begins to rise back across the spur you tackled lower down. As the road sweeps around the spur, the gradient relents in stages. A sharp bend to the right gives a more direct ascent of the hill. Beyond the copse of trees to the right, this slackens to a very gentle climb which tops out at the lone tree beside the rough track for Evelick Cottage.

A welcome drop to the ruins of Evelick Castle ensues, with a softer descent as the road sweeps right past Evelick Farm. The return to climbing is equally benign as the road cuts across farmland on approach to the narrow passage through the valley. As it makes its way through the narrows, the road steepens at the passing places. A gentle bend beyond a final passing place affords a more open aspect and the road soon tops out at the head of the valley.

15

DUNDEE LAW DUNDEE

Distance 1.4 miles/2.2km
Total Height Gain 525ft/160m
Altitude Range 36-561ft/11-171m
Average Gradient 7.2%
Start Road junction – Meadowside Street and Panmure Street (NO 403305)
End War Memorial (NO 392313)
Map OS Landranger 54
Rail Dundee Station (<1 mile)

Brace yourself for the merciless wall of tarmac that leads to the aptly named Hilltown on this climb from bustling city centre to prominent airy landmark.

There's nothing cultured about this brute of a climb which sets out from the junction of Meadowside and Panmure Street on the northern side of the city's central retail district, with The McManus, Dundee's Art Gallery and Museum, at your back.

Take the middle lane signed for Forfar from the outset, and pedal gently up to the junction with Meadow Lane. The gradient starts to kick in as the road passes the multi-storey car park on the right to reach traffic lights at a T-junction. Turn right to join Victoria Road (A929), immediately slipping into the left-hand lane signed for Hilltown and Forfar.

There's a brief let-up on approach to another set of traffic lights, but don't be fooled. You now turn left to be confronted with Hilltown, a straight section of road rising ferociously up the hill. Although it is a convex climb, the statistics that tell you on paper the gradient is easing don't count – you won't feel it – and the ascent remains taxing throughout.

On the first pitch, up to the kink to the right at McDonald Street, there is a railing to assist pedestrians – cyclists must go it alone. Severe climbing persists to the bus stop across from a car park on the right. Beyond, it's a stiff rather than severe ascent

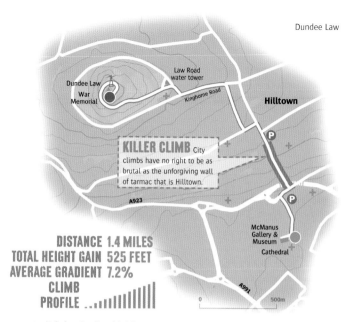

KILLER CLIMB City climbs have no right to be as brutal as the unforgiving wall of tarmac that is Hilltown.

DISTANCE 1.4 MILES
TOTAL HEIGHT GAIN 525 FEET
AVERAGE GRADIENT 7.2%
CLIMB PROFILE .....ııııllllll

– scant relief after that first thigh-busting pitch – to reach a set of traffic lights. Proper respite follows as the incline drops further to reach another set of traffic lights, where the one-way system forces you left into Constitution Street.

Take the first right to join Rosebank Street, with the first of three signs directing you to Dundee Law. The gradient ramps up on approach to the kink to the right at Stirling Street and again just beyond, continuing to a T-junction. Turn left along Kinghorne Road for a view ahead to the summit. At the junction with Carmichael Street to the left and Bruce Street to the right, carry on ahead to glide (relatively) effortlessly up to the signed turn-off at Law Road.

Don't let yourself be lulled into the idea that the difficulties are all past. Stiffer climbing resumes after turning right and continues through the signed turn-off to the left, passing the watertower (disguised as an old Scots doocot) around the bend. A brutal straight hauls the road up to the bus turning area, where the road narrows and the surface quality deteriorates. An initial transition to gentler climbing lasts only up until a passing place. Thereafter, the road winds its way up around the upper slopes to finally reach the war memorial, with uninterrupted 360° views over Fife, Angus and all corners of the city of Dundee.

17

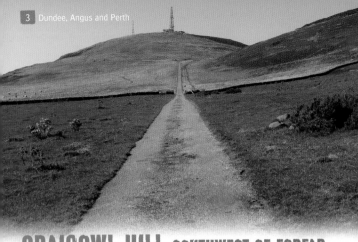

CRAIGOWL HILL SOUTHWEST OF FORFAR

Distance 2.4 miles/3.8km
Total Height Gain 1043ft/318m
Altitude Range 440-1476ft/134-450m
Average Gradient 8.3%
Start Road junction (NO 395377)
End Road end (NO 377400)
Map OS Landranger 54
Rail Dundee Station (5 miles)

The triple attractions of a closed road, 1000ft of ascent and the top-of-the-world feeling that comes from gaining the summit of the region's highest hill make this a must-do climb.

Craigowl Hill dominates the Tayside skyline and projects an imperial presence over its foothills. The low point on the road to Craigowl is at the crossing of the Fithie Burn, but this route starts some 0.4 miles of barely perceptible climbing further on by the track junction to Balnuith.

The ascent becomes more marked from the left-hand bend that separates the opening straights, and continues stiffly around the gentle S-bend that follows. As the road straightens, it summits and drops gently to the crossroads.

Continue ahead on a no-through road, signed for Hillside of Prieston. After rising gradually away from the junction, the road narrows to single track where the gradient picks up on passing beneath an overhead line, only to pull back again on approach to a sweeping left-hand bend. A long straight follows, with the gentle climbing persisting through another left-hand bend and the start of the next straight.

A distinctive lone tree to the left signals a return to a more challenging incline. This persists through more long straights, each divided by gentle right-hand bends that carry the road up to the road/track

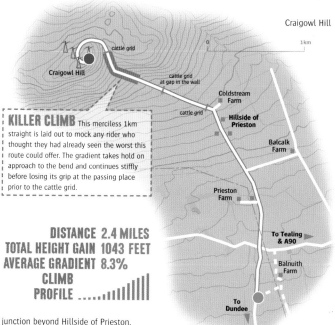

0   1km

KILLER CLIMB This merciless 1km straight is laid out to mock any rider who thought they had already seen the worst this route could offer. The gradient takes hold on approach to the bend and continues stiffly before losing its grip at the passing place prior to the cattle grid.

DISTANCE 2.4 MILES
TOTAL HEIGHT GAIN 1043 FEET
AVERAGE GRADIENT 8.3%
CLIMB
PROFILE ......ııllı

junction beyond Hillside of Prieston.

Keep left at the fork to soon meet a gate, which is normally locked and demands a dismount. If open, take care at the cattle grid, which is buckled, with farm dirt another likely hazard on this road. These inconveniences are quickly forgotten as the prospect of a remorseless straight 1km of climbing beckons. The first of 13 bricked bunkers is soon passed, from which point it's a steady ascent until the road cuts through a gap in the wall. Here, traverse the raised cattle grid that sits aside the usually unlocked gate. Climbing ramps up beyond the fourth salt bunker, steepening further on approach to the next and only easing back before it reaches the sixth.

You'll still be feeling the burn in your legs as the straight gives way to a sweeping right-hand bend. Now heading away from the summit towards the col on its shoulder, the pain finally eases as you meet a passing place on the right. However, with more sadistic tricks up its sleeve, the gradient ramps up again after another cattle grid with a short stiff climb around a left-hand bend. Now working your way around Craigowl's northern side, there is some respite before the climbing resumes with renewed vigour as the road curls up to the transmitter through a series of left-hand bends, each of which ramps up the difficulty.

CATERTHUNS NORTHWEST OF BRECHIN

Distance 2.1 miles/3.3km
Total Height Gain 614ft/187m
Altitude Range 210-794ft/64-242m
Average Gradient 5.6%
Start Bridge (NO 573636)
End Parking place (NO 552661)
Map OS Landranger 44
Rail Montrose Station (11 miles)

Whatever you do, don't be fooled by the gentle start as the route follows this up with a morale-draining series of short sharp climbs and dips, finishing the weary combatant off with a stiff ascent to the summit.

Climb away from the bridge to enter Balrownie on a gentle right-hand bend. The gradient eases on the straight run through this small settlement before a slight drop down to a right-hand bend precedes another straight rise. Although bordered by high farm hedges on either side, the summit road can be viewed ahead. After passing the track to Balrownie Farm, the road dips gently to a right-hand bend, then levels out on approach to a junction.

Ignore the main road bending left for a stiff climb on the narrow single-track road ahead, now hemmed in by banks and hedging, particularly on the right. There's a marked let-up in gradient for a short straight, passing the gas station on the left, before a steep dip to a right-hand bend.

Now slashing its way between forest to the left and steep banking to the right, the climb from the bottom of the dip comprises three bends (left, left, right) dividing short straights. A more gentle section leads to the high hedgerows of West Muirside where the road levels on approach to a crossroads.

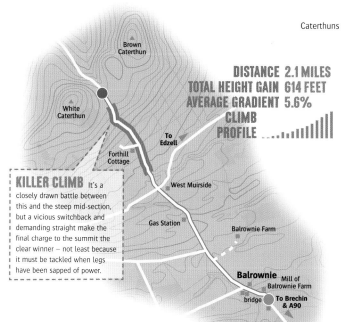

DISTANCE 2.1 MILES
TOTAL HEIGHT GAIN 614 FEET
AVERAGE GRADIENT 5.6%
CLIMB
PROFILE

Brown
Caterthun

White
Caterthun

To
Edzell

Forthill
Cottage

West Muirside

Gas Station

Balrownie Farm

Balrownie Mill of
Balrownie Farm

bridge **To Brechin
& A90**

KILLER CLIMB It's a closely drawn battle between this and the steep mid-section, but a vicious switchback and demanding straight make the final charge to the summit the clear winner – not least because it must be tackled when legs have been sapped of power.

0   1km

Give way and go directly over the crossroads with care as vision is obscured here. A brisk climb follows, weaving right, then left, before dropping briefly. This marks the start of an unforgiving ascent to the summit, with a sharp rise immediately after the dip. A series of bends (right, left, right) is followed by a longer straight, with two gentle left-hand bends breaking up two further long straights (the first at Forthill cottage) on approach to the upper hillside.

A sharper left-hand bend signals the most challenging, and thankfully final, part of your assault on the hillside – by now, you'll find little left in your reserve tank. Starting with a switchback to the right, the stiff gradient is maintained up through a sweeping left-hand bend to the summit car park on the straight beyond.

Antiquarians may reward themselves with a short stroll up to the summits of Brown and White Caterthun to see the remains of the Iron Age forts, where laid out below the agricultural landscape of Angus drifts to the coast and the upland wilderness of the Angus Glens. Having come this far, it might also prove too tempting to resist the delights of the mile-long 7% climb on the other side of the hill.

3
Fraserburgh

Tomintoul
4

2
ABERDEEN

Banchory

1

Nowhere in Highland Scotland is whittling down the best hillclimbs to a handful more of a challenge than in the North East. Is it possible to ignore the Slug Road near Stonehaven, the venue for the competitive hillclimbs of Deeside Thistle CC? Or the motorway-like expanse of the A93 on its brutal climb up to the Cairnwell Ski Resort? The walls of tarmac that rear up from the coast at Pennan, Crovie and Cullen? Or either of the fierce ascents away from the Bridge of Brown? And what about the gruelling climbs to the bealach on the A939 between Gairnshiel and Corgarff – surely these must be worthy of selection?

Well, no, not in light of the competition. The inclusion of the Lecht, the giant of the final four, is surely incontestable. The classic ascent from Clatterin' Brig to Cairn o' Mount, where the quality of the climbing experience is only matched by sublime summit views, must likewise be near the top of every Highland hillclimber's list. If –

as here – you were to include just one of the North East's famous coastal climbs, meanwhile, it would be difficult to justify passing over the vertigo-inducing ascent from Gardenstown in favour of any of its competitors.

The inclusion of Brimmond Hill on the outskirts of Aberdeen – a tough climb through a forested estate, managed countryside and open moorland with unparalleled views of the North's largest city – may be more contentious. But where would be the fun without a bit of lively debate – see what you think?

ABERDEEN TO THE GRAMPIANS

CAIRN O' MOUNT CLATTERIN' BRIG

Distance 2.1 miles/3.4km
Total Height Gain 1068ft/326m
Altitude Range 408-1476ft/125-450m
Average Gradient 9.6%
Start Bridge (NO 665782)
End Upper car park (NO 649807)
Map OS Landranger 45
Rail Laurencekirk Station (9 miles)

A tough climb on a good quality road which starts severely and ends stiffly, with the gentler intervening ascent over wild moorland only slightly alleviating the pain.

If the snow gates at the foot of the ascent offer a subtle warning of what lies ahead, the road sign spells it out – an initial gradient of 16% away from the Clatterin' Brig makes this a climb not to be messed with. On the bright side, the initial slope is convex, with the climb becoming more

bearable as the gradient relents in stages.

After a very steep opening pitch and initial left-hand bend, the start of the snow poles to the left signal a welcome slackening of gradient, easing up further on the fern-lined straight that follows. This is rudely interrupted by a Z-bend with rougher road quality to contend with, before another long straight with views to the heather-clad hillside on the left. The gradient relaxes further as you approach a right-hand bend, with more obvious respite before the next left-hand bend. From here, the road climbs stiffly, but not severely, bypassing a distinctive ruin to the left and topping out just before a track branching to the right.

You're now almost midway, with the road clambering much more gently around the hillside through five right-hand bends, each interspersed by straights. A change of direction after a left-hand bend (with an old

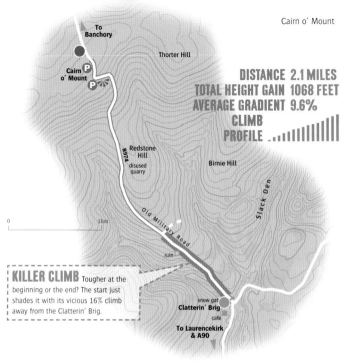

DISTANCE 2.1 MILES
TOTAL HEIGHT GAIN 1068 FEET
AVERAGE GRADIENT 9.6%
CLIMB
PROFILE

KILLER CLIMB Tougher at the beginning or the end? The start just shades it with its vicious 16% climb away from the Clatterin' Brig.

quarry to the right) brings a clear view of the final charge up to the Cairn o' Mount summit. The foot of this ascent is approached on a long stretch of road, broken by two bends (left, then right).

The road steepens on approach to the right-hand bend at the foot of the summit climb, after the central road markings begin. A wide sweep to the left follows through three left-hand bends with just a slight slackening of gradient after the first. The next (fourth) bend to the left, approaching the viewpoint car park, is

actually a switchback. Avoid the temptation to stop here for the views just now, and instead continue to the upper summit, starting with a sharp 90° turn to the right. The severity of this final climb persists through a left-hand bend, ending at a right-hand bend where the summit roadside car park starts. The true summit is at the far end of the car park and is reached by a gentle climb. It is worth returning to the lower viewpoint to savour what you have scaled before heading all the way back down.

25

BRIMMOND HILL WEST OF ABERDEEN

Distance 2.2 miles/3.5km
Total Height Gain 630ft/192m
Altitude Range 230-853ft/70-260m
Average Gradient 5.5%
Start Dyce Drive roundabout on A96
(NJ 879107)
End Rise on approach to road end at lower
transmitter (NJ 857092)
Map OS Landranger 38
Rail Dyce Station (3 miles)

**Although there are longer climbs and
steeper pitches to reach the summit car
park on Brimmond Hill, this route is less
troubled by traffic and offers the most
height gain per mile.**

Leave the A96 at Dyce Drive roundabout
and climb gently through a right-hand bend
to enter the Scottish Agricultural Centre's
Craibstone Estate. The twin-track road is
tree-lined throughout and there are several

sleeping policemen to negotiate. Now
under the trees, a short level straight is
followed by a left-hand bend and some
gradual climbing.

The first of the steeper pitches starts from
the second right-hand bend after the
straight. Bear to the left with right of way at
the junction, the steep gradient persisting
until you come to the zebra crossing at the
right-hand bend just after the turn-off for
the Ferguson Building.

A now much gentler gradient is countered
by a narrower, rougher road until open
aspect is reached. Leave the estate behind
at a staggered junction, turning left, then
right, signed for the Brimmond Bistro.

Following a good quality single-track
road, the middle section of the route starts
with a stiff climb on the straight, bordered
– but not hemmed in – by a tall hedge to
the left. The gradient eases back beyond

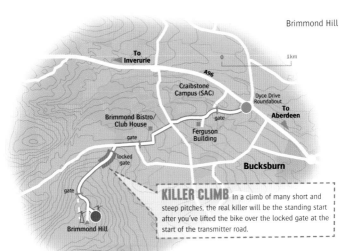

To Inverurie

A96

Craibstone
Campus (SAC)

Dyce Drive
Roundabout

To Aberdeen

Brimmond Bistro/
Club House

gate

Ferguson
Building

gate

locked
gate

gate

Bucksburn

Brimmond Hill

KILLER CLIMB In a climb of many short and steep pitches, the real killer will be the standing start after you've lifted the bike over the locked gate at the start of the transmitter road.

DISTANCE 2.2 MILES
TOTAL HEIGHT GAIN 630 FEET
AVERAGE GRADIENT 5.5%
CLIMB
PROFILE

the hedge and around the sharp left-hand bend before the road drops gradually to another sharp turn, this time to the right, on a rougher surface.

Road quality improves with the return to climbing. Pass through a gate which you'll usually find open to reach a junction at the bend of a minor road. Give way if necessary as you continue ahead on a steady ascent to the Brimmond Hill car park, just as the forest ends on the right. Turn left here.

The climb to the summit comprises four pitches, with eleven drains crossing the road at intervals exacerbating the difficulties. The first pitch is the steepest

and longest, and you may find yourself cursing at the gate (usually locked) which you'll need to hoist the bike over for a standing start to the stiff climb up the spur. This bends to the left, then right. The gradient slackens at the right-hand bend, but only really pulls back at a left-hand bend further on. This easier climbing is replaced on the next straight by a second, shorter steep pitch, followed by some brief respite at a stand of trees.

Beyond the upper gate (closed but usually unlocked), climb stiffly away on a left-hand bend and along a straight, the gradient easing back after rounding a right-hand bend. There is a minor dip on the straight that follows before a left-hand bend marks the start of the fourth and final pitch. On reaching a fork in the road, bear left to head towards the lower transmitter. The road tops out before dropping down to its gates.

27

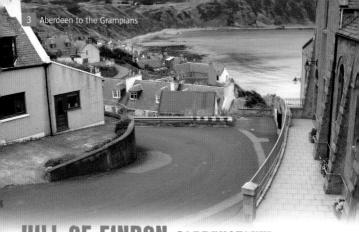

HILL OF FINDON GARDENSTOWN

Distance 1.33 miles/2.1km
Total Height Gain 512ft/156m
Altitude Range 13-525ft/4-160m
Average Gradient 7.3%
Start Road junction, Harbour Street and New Ground (NJ 801649)
End Road bend at entrance to Bonnieview (NJ 798636)
Map OS Landranger 29
Rail Huntly Station (29 miles)

Despite those wafting harbour smells and the sea breeze tugging at your back, there will be little thought in your head but the bends on this route up through 'Gamrie' or Gardenstown. The staged reduction in gradient is scant relief for the severity of your initial efforts on what can only be described as a cliff climb. Sheer madness!

Protected from the ravages of the Moray Firth by a line of industrial buildings, reinventing themselves now that the fishing industry has all but gone, the short but savage climb up to the Hill of Findon starts at the junction with Harbour Street. A stiff but mercifully short initial pitch eases off at the junction with Harbour Road to the right, but there is no respite beyond as the road twists its way steeply up towards the junction with Main Street.

The difficulty ramps up on approach to what transpires to be a switchback to the left, hidden from view by housing on the bend – the inside bend is best avoided if possible. Again, you'll find little relief beyond the steep pitch as the road heads onward and upward towards a left-hand bend, where it sweeps majestically around and above the back of the same houses. Crash barriers heighten the dramatic impact and, strangely, do not seem out of place in such a built-up area. No sooner has the climb exited the sweep to the left, than it

KILLER CLIMB A savage start to an airy cliff climb with no let-up until the end of Gamrie Brae. Not even the sea air will revive you as this winding road negotiates a few tight switchbacks and a jumble of bends to reach the foot of the brae.

DISTANCE 1.33 MILES
TOTAL HEIGHT GAIN 512 FEET
AVERAGE GRADIENT 7.3%
CLIMB
PROFILE

enters a staged switchback to the right, passing the imposing edifice of Gardenstown Church, with the brutal gradient persisting through the bend.

As the bend is finally rounded, this eases back to a stiff climb, but, alas, it's all too brief. From the first cottage in the row on the right, the gradient increases once more as the road winds up along a series of short straights interspersed with gentle bends to reach the next section of the climb.

Gamrie Brae is approached with a switchback to the left that takes the road around the distinctive coastguard station on the inside bend of the turn. Although not the steepest stretch in this tangle of tarmac, the Brae is the most imposing, rising up and across the hill for a 250m straight.

On reaching the wide expanse of road at the end of the straight, swing sharply to the right, continuing on the B9123 rather in the direction of Crovie on Bracoden Road. What follows is an even longer straight, albeit one on which the ascent becomes progressively less taxing, with the climbing easing after Bayview Road and then again on reaching the Gamrie Brae nursing home.

The village is left behind at the end of the straight, as a steeper pitch kicks in, veering to the right, then left to reach open countryside. Beyond this gentle Z-bend, the route continues to rise at a more humane level, weaving its way up to top out at Bonnieview cottage.

THE LECHT COCK BRIDGE, UPPER DON VALLEY

Distance 1.9 miles/3.1km
Total Height Gain 883ft/269m
Altitude Range 1309-2113ft/399-644m
Average Gradient 8.6%
Start Bridge (NJ 257092)
End Road/track junction (NJ 252119)
Map OS Landranger 37
Rail Huntly Station (35 miles), Carrbridge Station (32 miles)

So you've survived the remorseless Allargue ... only to find a reviving dip downhill is followed by the grinding Lecht Road with many hidden tricks as it ploughs on up towards the ski station.

The road rises majestically away from the bridge over the River Don, sweeping to the left as it passes the Allargue Arms Hotel. To say that the gradient eases after this bend would be technically accurate, but it won't offer any relief as the stiff climbing

continues unabated through the straight and the right-hand bend beyond. Although you will still be pumping hard on the pedals, there is another 'relative' easing back of the incline as the road passes through the snow gates. Now the difficulty rises a few notches on a switchback bend to the left, with a rougher surface on the straight that follows doing little to assist.

The end of this most murderous of climbs is in sight as you reach the first of two right-hand bends, the second of which swings past a large car park. It is tempting to stop and gape at the view, but it might be better to avoid a standing start from here. The road now wriggles a short distance to the top of the Hill of Allargue, which is reached without any jeering false summits.

In a just world, this would be job over. However, this is the Lecht and from the summit of Allargue, the daunting prospect

DISTANCE 1.9 MILES
TOTAL HEIGHT GAIN 883 FEET
AVERAGE GRADIENT 8.6%
CLIMB PROFILE

KILLER CLIMB The road sign warning of a 20% gradient at the start is unnecessary – Allargue makes no attempt to disguise the brutality of the climb along its four straights, a switchback and a sweeping swing up to the summit.

of the climb up the spur of Little Corr Riabhach is presented. At least there is some respite in the form of an initial descent, though it is best not to dwell on the fact that everything lost has to be regained on the climb ahead. From the descent, it mistakenly appears that the climb ahead consists of three parts, but many false summits make for a less than straightforward climb.

Swing left at the foot of the ascent where a lulling rise precedes a brutal pitch up to a false summit. An extension – stiff but less severe – drags the road to a second false summit a short distance beyond. Two further false summits lie ahead, but there is a more marked easing back of the gradient between each – together these might be considered the start of the middle section of this climb. The fifth summit, just before a right-hand bend, is the real deal.

Some levelling around the bend steadies the legs before the final push up to Little Corr Riabhach. This begins with a steep straight pitch and is followed by three short straights between gentle bends (right, then left and left again) to top out at the track junction and a roadside parking place.

You can continue another half mile or so to the Lecht Ski Station, aesthetically the more fitting conclusion to the climb, though purists be warned – it's 16 feet lower!

31

Hillclimb challenges radiate in all directions from Inverness, the capital of Highland Scotland. The many roads that rear up from the city to the south present a varied mix of challenges, although the heavy traffic on the A9 trunk road is best avoided. The roads above Loch Ness to the southwest give more than their fair share of classic climbs, and the picturesque Black Isle to the north is not to be overlooked either.

South of Inverness, the solemn dome-like peaks of the Cairngorm plateau (the previous chapter makes brief forays into the Cairngorms from the east) form a playground for cyclists of all types. The Cairn Gorm Ski Road has emerged as a Scottish hillclimb favourite, itself one of Scotland's toughest hillclimb races but also the sting in the tail of the Cairngorm Classics Sportive.

To the west, Loch Ness plays host to the short sharp shock variety of hillclimbing. There is very little between Abriachan, Achtuie and Strone – each featuring an impossibly steep start and limited release from a vicious campaign of torture until the end. Of the three, the relentless assault

on the hillside at Achtuie wins out for being both steeper and, as a no-through road, more likely to be devoid of traffic – a welcome consideration when weaving across the road may be the only way to gain purchase on the steepest parts. The old military road to Carn an t-Suidhe, meanwhile, is a long haul, affording views of the loch and the Monadhliath mountains.

Rounding off the collection is the Heights of Dochcarty at Dingwall. Two pitches of purgatory are followed by a more conciliatory angle, topping out in the foothills of Ben Wyvis, a vast, sprawling landmark which will surely assume near-heavenly status after the torment that precedes it.

Dingwall

INVERNESS

Drumnadrochit

Aviemore

Fort Augustus

AROUND INVERNESS

CAIRN GORM SKI ROAD GLENMORE

Distance 3.67 miles/5.9km
Total Height Gain 994ft/303m
Altitude Range 1073-2067ft/327-630m
Average Gradient 5.1%
Start Road bend (NH 981091)
End Height marker at the mountain railway base station (NH 990060)
Map OS Landranger 36
Rail Aviemore Station (5 miles)

The free-ranging reindeer that roam these bare hills will be the last thing on your mind as you emerge from a stiff climb through Glenmore Forest to tackle the ascent to the Cairn Gorm ski station.

From the last houses of Glenmore, sweep right to cross the Abhainn Ruigh-eunachan, which flows into Loch Morlich, where a gradual rise on the straight leads to a left-hand bend, taking you through the snow gates and into the forest proper. The lower half of this forest climb is gentle with long straights interrupted by wide, sweeping bends. The straight after the snow gates is followed by a broad curve to the right at the turn-off to a picnic area. Beyond this, two right-hand bends are quickly followed by a sharper left-hand bend and the road flattens very briefly to cross a bridge.

Although the climb away from the bridge on the upper part of the forest ascent is not overly taxing, the gradient now cranks up in stages, with harder pushes on the pedals needed beyond the first bend, just after three roadside boulders.

The gradient stiffens much more overtly at the foot of the long approach to the switchback to the left, easing around the bend as the road deviates eastwards to find an easy route up the steep lower reaches of the An t-Aonach spur. Despite the detour, the road steepens at the first right-hand bend beyond the switchback, continuing at this incline on the straight that follows,

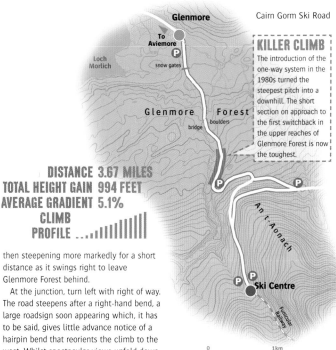

Glenmore

To Aviemore

P

snow gates

Loch Morlich

Glenmore   Forest

bridge

boulders

P

P

P

P   **Ski Centre**

An t-Aonach

Funicular Railway

0   1km

KILLER CLIMB
The introduction of the one-way system in the 1980s turned the steepest pitch into a downhill. The short section on approach to the first switchback in the upper reaches of Glenmore Forest is now the toughest.

**DISTANCE 3.67 MILES
TOTAL HEIGHT GAIN 994 FEET
AVERAGE GRADIENT 5.1%
CLIMB
PROFILE**

then steepening more markedly for a short distance as it swings right to leave Glenmore Forest behind.

At the junction, turn left with right of way. The road steepens after a right-hand bend, a large roadsign soon appearing which, it has to be said, gives little advance notice of a hairpin bend that reorients the climb to the west. Whilst spectacular views unfold down across the hillside to Loch Morlich in the foreground and Aviemore behind, the tarmac continues to rise stiffly up to a false summit on the immediate horizon at a left-hand bend. The road hugs the hillside as it works its way around the spur, the gradient easing as it resumes its southerly bearing and continues towards a road junction.

Ignore the give way signs, as traffic only heads downhill on the road to the right. Turn left for a stiff climb to a false summit where the ski centre comes into full view. Now a more gradual ascent takes you

through the boulders at the entrance to the car park, easing back halfway up. The road summits at the log barrier that doubles as a height marker beside the base station of the ski tow and mountain railway. Should you be experiencing any elation on having hauled yourself up this far, you can bring yourself back down to earth with the thought that from here passengers can rise 1500ft – or 50% higher than the climb you have just inflicted on yourself – in as little as five minutes!

35

CARN AN T-SUIDHE FORT AUGUSTUS

Distance 5 miles/8km
Total Height Gain 1388ft/423m
Altitude Range 59-1289ft/18-393m
Average Gradient 5.3%
Start Road/path junction (NH 382084)
End Viewpoint/summit car park
(NH 449104)
Map OS Landranger 34
Rail Inverness Station (33 miles),
Spean Bridge (23 miles)

You'll need grit and determination for this punishing boot camp on one of General Wade's military roads, where four pitches are rolled into a long hillclimb with more than 1000ft in net height gain.

Starting on the shores of Loch Ness at the junction with the path for Ardachy Bridge, this monster of a climb follows the B862 for its entire length. A nice gentle rise is soon swallowed by the increasing gradient as it rears up on approach to a sweeping left-hand bend to start the climb into the forested eastern slopes of Glen Albyn. Passing a minor road junction at the bend, the climb continues stiffly on the straight beyond. Two sharp bends (right, then left), separated by a short straight, swing the road past a works entrance before it continues northeast again. From here, a series of straights and ten bends carry the tarmac up and up with no option of taking your mind off the grind with any Nessie-spotting, should you even be capable of shifting your focus from the road ahead, as the forest cover on the downslope gives few glimpses of the loch below. The end is in sight when the sequence of alternate right/left bends is replaced by a pair of right-hand bends carrying the

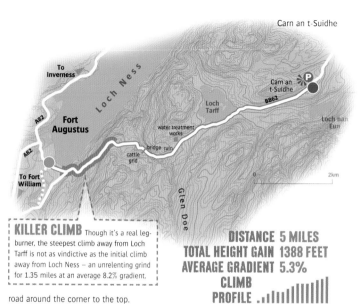

Carn an t-Suidhe

To Inverness

Loch Ness

Carn an t-Suidhe

B862

Loch Tarff

Fort Augustus

water treatment works

Loch nan Eun

A82

bridge ruin

cattle grid

To Fort William

Glen Doe

0   2km

KILLER CLIMB Though it's a real leg-burner, the steepest climb away from Loch Tarff is not as vindictive as the initial climb away from Loch Ness – an unrelenting grind for 1.35 miles at an average 8.2% gradient.

DISTANCE 5 MILES
TOTAL HEIGHT GAIN 1388 FEET
AVERAGE GRADIENT 5.3%
CLIMB
PROFILE ..il llll lllll

road around the corner to the top.

A left-hand bend marks the start of the descent, now heading eastwards. Initially steep, this bottoms out, with a gentle rise towards the end of the straight. After a right-hand bend, it weaves more gently down the hill, crossing a cattle grid before sweeping around two left-hand bends to bottom out and cross a stone bridge in Glen Doe.

Some stiff climbing follows, swerving to the left around the hillside before following a Z-bend under the shadow of a ruin on the hill above. This relaxes to a gentle climb on the straight that follows before rearing up at the right-hand bend just after the works entrance. The second left-hand bend after this marks the point where the gradient pulls back, with a gradual ascent to reach the shores of Loch Tarff.

A pleasant meander on an undulating lochside road allows for some regrouping before the final push. This begins as soon as you leave the water's edge with the steepest pitch in the whole expedition. Mercifully short, the leg burn ends when the pitch tops out at a left-hand bend after an initial swing to the right.

Gentler climbing follows as the road winds up to a straight where it levels out before rising again at the left-hand bend beyond. The summit is reached after three straights – the first comprises many changes in gradient and the second contains a false summit. The true summit lies a little way beyond, around a left-hand bend at the viewpoint and car park.

ACHTUIE DRUMNADROCHIT

Distance 1 mile/1.6km
Total Height Gain 702ft/214m
Altitude Range 118-820ft/36-250m
Average Gradient 13.6%
Start Road junction, A82/minor
(NH 517302)
End Crossroads (NH 521313)
Map OS Landranger 26
Rail Inverness Station (15 miles),
Spean Bridge (41 miles)

**There's no arguing with the statistics –
this merciless mile-long assault on the
hillside by the banks of Loch Ness is one
of Scotland's toughest road climbs.**

This climb up to Achtuie is also one of
Scotland's hidden gems – one statute mile of
purgatory on a little travelled road of
impeccable quality. For the most part, the
tarmac follows the course of the forested river

valley that drops down from Loch Glanaidh.

The start is innocuous enough as the
northbound road signed for Drumbuie
climbs steadily away from the junction with
the A82, just to the east of Drumnadrochit.
However, lurking in the overgrowth is a
roadsign warning of the 20% gradient
ahead. What follows does not disappoint –
the incline picks up sharply as the road
weaves to the right, then left on passing
Drumbuie Farm.

The brutal gradient persists beyond the
track junction headed for Lower Drumbuie
to the left. Incredibly, on reaching the
second passing place on the left beyond
the junction, the climb steepens further.
Gears and thighs will be strained to the
limit and the granny gear will swiftly
become a necessity, rather than a luxury.
A stiff straight is followed by a Z-bend

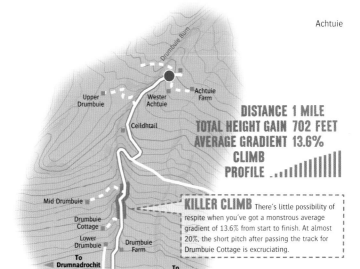

DISTANCE 1 MILE
TOTAL HEIGHT GAIN 702 FEET
AVERAGE GRADIENT 13.6%
CLIMB
PROFILE ....

KILLER CLIMB There's little possibility of respite when you've got a monstrous average gradient of 13.6% from start to finish. At almost 20%, the short pitch after passing the track for Drumbuie Cottage is excruciating.

without any let-up from the climb.

After the track leading to Mid-Drumbuie, just beyond a passing place to the left, the hill finally releases its grip just a little. However, this is little more than a shift from an 'hors categorie' to a Cat 4 climb. The ascent remains taxing up to the right-hand bend at the end of the straight, maintaining a gradient of almost 16%.

As the road swings southeastwards, moving away from the forested river valley into more open countryside, the incline weakens. Continue with right of way at the junction where the road bends sharply left, and return to tough climbing. After a brief straight, at another left bend the climb intensifies again.

There is an easing in severity at the bend beyond the white cottage of Ceildhtail, although the climbing remains taxing until you come to the false summit at the passing place on a long straight. The ascent beyond is less savage, right up to the point under the telegraph pole just after the fenced square on the right-hand side.

From here to the top it's a challenging climb once more. It first picks up on approach to the right-hand bend and continues on the straight that follows.

There is an easing of gradient as the road reaches the crash barriers that keep you from the heavily eroded side of the valley. Stiffer climbing returns on approach to a final bend to the right and remains tough on the ensuing straight up to the crossroads at the end.

HEIGHTS OF DOCHCARTY DINGWALL

Distance 1.9 miles/3km
Total Height Gain 748ft/228m
Altitude Range 23-748ft/7-228m
Average Gradient 7.6%
Start Road junction (NH 539598)
End Road/track junction (NH 528623)
Map OS Landranger 20/26
Rail Dingwall Station (<1 mile)

There can be few places in Scotland where a wall of tarmac at 12% is but a prelude to the main event.

Leaving the road junction, follow a sharp right-hand bend for the gentle, lulling climb up to the roadsign. There is not the remotest possibility of flouting the speed limit on the wall of single-track tarmac that now stretches up and up for the next half a mile. Under the forest canopy, it's a steep ascent – and steeper still – on a concave slope that eases to a stiff climb after the first passing place. This pattern is repeated with a steep and steepening concave slope stretching up from the second passing place to the first gates of the villas after the crossroads, followed by an easing of the gradient to a stiff climb to the last gate. From here, the road steepens and rises fiercely for the remainder of the straight.

The road only flattens after it rounds the 90° left-hand bend, widening to twin track and emerging into open countryside. Make the most of this chance to recover from the shock of the initial exertion, as the gradient soon ramps up as it sweeps 45° at a right-hand bend.

Keep legal and take the 90° right-hand bend at the kerbside. From nowhere, the tarmac seems to rise up to face level and the road is imprisoned once more by trees.

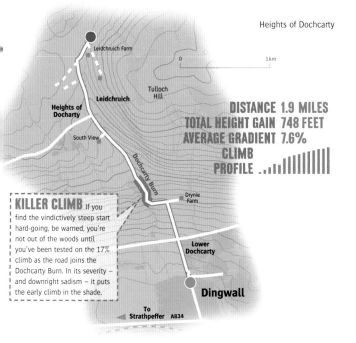

Leidchruich Farm

Tulloch Hill

Leidchruich

Heights of Dochcarty

South View

Dochcarty Burn

Drynie Farm

DISTANCE 1.9 MILES
TOTAL HEIGHT GAIN 748 FEET
AVERAGE GRADIENT 7.6%
CLIMB
PROFILE

KILLER CLIMB If you find the vindictively steep start hard-going, be warned, you're not out of the woods until you've been tested on the 17% climb as the road joins the Dochcarty Burn. In its severity — and downright sadism — it puts the early climb in the shade.

Lower Dochcarty

Dingwall

To Strathpeffer A834

An energy-sapping gradient is maintained through a sharp left-hand bend and up the straight that lies beyond to reach a distinctive lone tree on the right. From here to the point at which it emerges out of the forest, the gradient eases to a mere severe climb! A more modest ascent to the next passing place may offer respite, but the road is also now more exposed to the wind.

The incline of the road, single-track once more, eases more markedly between passing places. The gradient stiffens beyond the upper passing place, though thankfully to a slope that is much less severe than the initial ascents. It eases further at the right-

hand bend before the junction.

Turn off the road, ploughing straight on ahead to rise steadily towards rougher countryside. Three long straights climb evenly, separated by sweeping bends to the right and then left. These bring the road to a sharper right-hand bend beyond the second track junction to the left. The road now rises more gradually to an obvious right-hand bend, after which it flattens on approach to the final straight. With Ben Wyvis dominating the horizon, the road curves gently left, and a steep but short straight is the last push before the torture ends at the road/track junction.

Toil and trouble are part and parcel of road hillclimbing – but if the delights of the northernmost reaches of Scotland are to be enjoyed (or endured) then for anyone living outwith these areas that toil must first be directed towards doing your research. These remote outposts are well beyond the reach of a day excursion from the Central Belt, and meticulous planning, not to mention significant quantities of pounds and pence, will be required to realise the dream of cycling on some of the most wildly scenic metalled roads in the UK. Therein lies the answer to the inevitable question: 'Is it worth the effort?'

In truth, there is not an abundance of hills to conquer and some of those that look good on paper turn out to be less appealing on the road (for one, the rough surface at Glen Loth discourages you from what, in profile, appears to be a fine climb). However, what this part of Scotland offers is many miles of traffic-light roads and a few hillclimb challenges so spectacular that the travel and cost considerations fade.

This chapter describes how to reach the highest point on Orkney direct from the centre of its capital, scale the infamous Berriedale Braes, the scourge of LEJOG

cyclists and HGVs alike, and ramp up the twin escarpments that lie beneath the towering crags of Quinag on its northern ascent from Unapool. The icing on the cake is the climb up to the summit of Saxa Vord, the most northerly road in the UK, which starts at the end of the 3700-mile long North Sea Cycle Route (EuroVelo route 12).

SUTHERLAND, ORKNEY AND SHETLAND

BERRIEDALE BRAES NORTH OF HELMSDALE

Distance South: 0.9 miles/1.4km.
North: 1.4 miles/2.3km
Total Height Gain South: 446ft/136m.
North: 541ft/165m
Altitude Range South: 36-482ft/11-147m.
North: 39-574ft/12-175m
Average Gradient South: 9.6%. North: 7.2%
Start South: Road/track junction (ND
119226).
North: Road bend on bridge (ND 119227)
End South: Road sign warning of deer
(ND 107217). North: Road bend on entering
Newport (ND 128242)
Map OS Landranger 17
Rail Helmsdale Station (9 miles)

**How do you like your pain? With
switchbacks, twists and turns or on long
straights of unrelenting ascent? The
infamous Berriedale Braes have it all!**

   South: The southern climb is the most
straightforward, but no less challenging for
that. Climb steeply away from the

road/track junction at the end of the bridge,
sweeping to the right to join a straight that
runs parallel to the escape lane for traffic
with failing brakes on the opposite side of
the road. Take care with the accumulation of
kerbside grit at this first bend. On passing a
salt bin, the road steepens further, this stiffer
gradient persisting around the Z-bend before
easing back at the passing place halfway
along the longer straight beyond. A
sweeping right-hand curve then brings the
road to the foot of the final and longest of
this climb's three straights, with the stiff
climbing lasting its full length. Beyond this
long, long stretch of torment, a left-hand
bend leads up to the roadsign that marks
the end of the climb. A further 115ft in
height can be gained over the next 1.5
miles, but the true summit of the climb is
best considered to be here at the transition
point between unremitting torture and
gentle, more relaxed tempo.

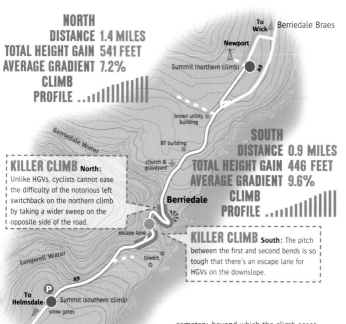

NORTH
DISTANCE 1.4 MILES
TOTAL HEIGHT GAIN 541 FEET
AVERAGE GRADIENT 7.2%
CLIMB
PROFILE ....

To Wick
Berriedale Braes

Newport

Summit (northern climb)

A9

brown utility building

BT building

SOUTH
DISTANCE 0.9 MILES
TOTAL HEIGHT GAIN 446 FEET
AVERAGE GRADIENT 9.6%
CLIMB
PROFILE ....

church & graveyard

Berriedale Water

Berriedale

KILLER CLIMB North:
Unlike HGVs, cyclists cannot ease the difficulty of the notorious left switchback on the northern climb by taking a wider sweep on the opposite side of the road.

escape lane

KILLER CLIMB South:
The pitch between the first and second bends is so tough that there's an escape lane for HGVs on the downslope.

Langwell Water

towers

A9

To Helmsdale

Summit (southern climb)

snow gates

0   500m

North: The northern climb starts by crossing the upward-slanting bridge over the Berriedale Water. Take a sharp right-hand bend to grind up the walled straight. Kink left before a tight switchback, again to the left, which is very steep on the climbing side. On the reverse straight, resist the temptation to stop for the views from the parking place on the left; instead swing around the right-hand bend to join another straight. The gradient eases on passing a house on the other side of the road, but only briefly – the stiffer climb resumes on passing a lone tree. After the straight, a Z-bend takes the road past a cemetery, beyond which the climb eases until it reaches a white BT utility building. Sweep to the right. Towards the end of this straight the gradient steepens again. A left-hand bend changes the direction of travel and the road continues to rise steeply to reach a brown utility building set back above it to the left. A little further on the climb levels at the road/track junction and then dips briefly to reach the turn-off for Newport. To reach the summit in this collection of houses 500ft above the sea, turn left and then veer right to join a long straight. Climbing is steeper near the foot of this and the short distance to the top is punctuated by a few false summits, each of which brings an easing back of the gradient.

45

WIDEFORD HILL KIRKWALL, ORKNEY ISLES

Distance 3 miles/4.8km
Total Height Gain 774ft/236m
Altitude Range 10-735ft/3-224m
Average Gradient 4.9%
Start Crossroads at junction of Main Street, A963 and A964 (HY 447105)
End Rise before road drops to transmitter (HY 412116)
Map OS Landranger 06
Ferry Kirkwall Ferry Terminal (<1 mile)

In clear weather the summit views are stunning, but only the hardened hillclimber will be in any state to bask in them after wrenching body and bike up Wideford's savage last mile.

Climb gently away from the crossroads with the A963 to follow the A964 in the direction of Orphir. After a double kink on the straight – right then left – the gradient steepens. Turn right just before the A964 bends sharp left to join Glaitness Road, headed for Stromness. The strain soon relents, with a long stretch of gentle climbing lasting for the remainder of the straight.

Gears should be ready for the steepening gradient at a sweeping left-hand bend from Soulisquoy Place and again to reach a right-hand bend. Now in open farmland, there is no real let-up until you come to Little Corse Cottage in the hamlet of Walliwall. The road sweeps right in Walliwall and then leaves it behind to face the first of two very long straights.

Climbing is gentle on this first of these, though there are some undulations. Beyond Walliwall quarry, stiffer climbing

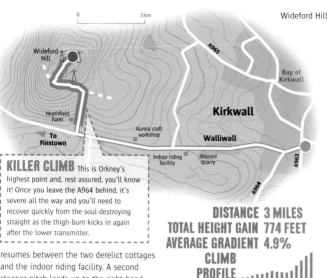

Wideford Hill

Heathfield Farm

To Finstown

A965

Bay of Kirkwall

Kirkwall

Aurora craft workshop

Walliwall

Indoor riding facility

disused quarry

A963

A964

KILLER CLIMB This is Orkney's highest point and, rest assured, you'll know it! Once you leave the A964 behind, it's severe all the way and you'll need to recover quickly from the soul-destroying straight as the thigh-burn kicks in again after the lower transmitter.

DISTANCE 3 MILES
TOTAL HEIGHT GAIN 774 FEET
AVERAGE GRADIENT 4.9%
CLIMB
PROFILE

resumes between the two derelict cottages and the indoor riding facility. A second steeper pitch leads up to the right-hand bend between the two straights. Beyond, the road flattens for a short way and then drops down in stages from the Aurora craft workshop to the hamlet below. There is an abrupt though thankfully brief return to climbing, lasting up to the turn-off to the right, signed for Wideford Cairn.

Turn right to join a single-track road. Savour the last few metres of gentle climbing up to Heathfield Farm, as this is followed by a brutal ramp on an unforgiving straight, the difficulty of which is likely to be compounded on its lower reaches by farm muck.

Hold out for the sharp left-hand bend at the top where a less severe climb offers some relief. There is a further easing back at the next left-hand bend, beyond which the road snakes its way up through soft

bends to reach the lower transmitter.

Veer more sharply to the left at this transmitter to join the foot of a steep straight, where the road quality improves and banks on both sides limit your exposure to the worst of the elements. Two right-hand bends lie ahead, the second a 90° turn away from a track junction. The gradient now kicks in harder, with a switchback to the right and a further left-hand bend separated by a short straight. Beyond the left-hand bend, the road aims straight for the summit, a few kinks breaking up the unrelenting slog of this direct approach. There is a very welcome easing back on approach to the summit, which is reached before the road drops down to the northeast transmitter.

SAXA VORD UNST, SHETLAND ISLANDS

Distance 2.3 miles/3.8km
Total Height Gain 896ft/273m
Altitude Range 36-919ft/11-280m
Average Gradient 7.2%
Start Road bend beyond bridge
(HP 637136)
End Transmitter gates (HP 633166)
Map OS Landranger 01
Ferry Belmont Ferry Terminal (11 miles)

This traffic-free ascent on a good quality road starts and ends stiffly with a bitterly exposed finale to Scotland's most northerly conquest.

You'll need to muster some Viking fire and an iron will to tackle this Norse giant, which stands at the tip of Unst's wild and starkly beautiful landscape, further north even than St Petersburg in Russia, and the site of the RAF's most northerly outpost during the Cold War.

Climb gently away from the road bend after the Burn of Norwick. The incline increases around a wide left-hand bend

before slackening to a gentle climb on the straight that follows. Beyond, a two-stage right-hand bend presents a stiffer climb, which also eases back on the straight beyond.

At a cattle grid, the climb savagely takes hold as you hoist your bike up the Housi Field escarpment to the stone bridge at the top – there is only fleeting relief between the first passing place and the sweeping left-hand bend on approach to the bridge.

Pull sharply away from the bridge to join a long straight, headed directly up to Sothers Field. The incline picks up slightly at two long passing places, maintaining this gradient around the left-hand bend at the top, past the White Heggie stone to the right on the straight beyond, and round the right-hand bend where the fence joins the roadside. It finally eases back at a false summit on the near horizon, by a gate.

Now cutting across the west side of Sothers Field, a short flat on approach to a right-hand bend gives glimpses of the sea

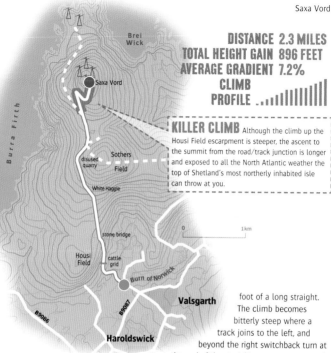

DISTANCE 2.3 MILES
TOTAL HEIGHT GAIN 896 FEET
AVERAGE GRADIENT 7.2%
CLIMB
PROFILE ...||||||||||

KILLER CLIMB Although the climb up the Housi Field escarpment is steeper, the ascent to the summit from the road/track junction is longer and exposed to all the North Atlantic weather the top of Shetland's most northerly inhabited isle can throw at you.

stacks of the Burra Firth and the Muggle Flugga lighthouse. Climb away from the bend, the slope easing back from the passing place at the old quarry to top out at the Sothers Field road junction. The summit climb now fills the horizon.

Dropping down from Sothers Field to the bealach shared with Saxa Vord, the ascent then begins gently where a path joins to the right – seize this chance to regroup as the gradient picks up after the lochans on the right where the road veers left to the

foot of a long straight. The climb becomes bitterly steep where a track joins to the left, and beyond the right switchback turn at the end of the straight you may even need to dismount to bypass a chain which sometimes spans the road.

The straight beyond presents a steady ascent with a brief let-up before steepening viciously around a wide bend to the left. On the subsequent straight, the climb remains taxing all the way to the summit, releasing you from its fiery clutches only after the left-hand bend just before the no-access gates. If you've managed to avoid a wind-battering on the way up, you're lucky – this spot holds Britain's highest unofficial wind speed record.

49

QUINAG UNAPOOL, ASSYNT

Distance 3.5 miles/5.6km
Total Height Gain 797ft/243m
Altitude Range 59-856ft/18-261m
Average Gradient 4.3%
Start Road bend beyond Maryck tearoom (NC 237327)
End Road bend on bealach (NC 236282)
Map OS Landranger 10
Rail Invershin or Lairg Station (41 miles)

Squeezed between a stiff climb away from Loch Glencoul and a gentle meandering drift towards the summit are two escarpments, each presenting a distinct but equally tough challenge.

Climb steadily away from the crash barriers at the first of three bends as the road snakes its way around the headland to reach the track leading to the Unapool House Holiday Cottages. Beyond, a right-hand bend drags the road away from the water and the climb stiffens. A long straight of unrelenting slog is broken by a left-hand bend at the Newton Lodge B&B sign before a second long straight pulls the road up past the junction for Newton. After easing back at a right-hand bend, the road winds its way gently up to the junction with the B869, signed for Lochinver.

A sharp climb away from the junction takes you towards the foot of the first escarpment. On rounding the corner to the left, the road steepens ever more to gain the escarpment, with six bends breaking up the monotony of the direct approach. The gradient finally slackens by a sheep pen on the left.

In the lull before the second escarpment, there's a kinder ascent as the road bends sharply to the left at the end of the straight. After crossing a river beyond another abrupt

KILLER CLIMB The upper escarpment with its switchback bend and 7.5% slope is, by a margin, tougher than its lower counterpart.

0   1km

DISTANCE 3.5 MILES
TOTAL HEIGHT GAIN 797 FEET
AVERAGE GRADIENT 4.3%
CLIMB
PROFILE ....ııllIIIll

left turn, the gradient eases further. A sharp turn to the right at the end of the next straight brings a brief return to climbing, but beyond a left-hand bend the route ahead is flat, with views towards the upper escarpment opening up. This gives you the much-needed opportunity to gather yourself for the final ascent – after a bend to the right it's a gentle roll up to the foot of the escarpment. Ahead in the small glen you'll see a waterfall before turning sharp right to cross the bridge and make your way up and across the base of the upper escarpment.

On rounding the switchback turn to the left halfway up, the incline steepens and remains challenging until the road curves right to pass through a cutting.

The highest point of the climb is reached by two long straights, separated by a gentle right-hand bend. Views down to Loch na Gainmhich can be enjoyed, as can close-ups of Quinag and Ghlas Bheinn when they are not shrouded in mist. The road steepens along the straight, although not dramatically, and the climb ends as it began – with gentle curves winding the road up to the summit on a left-hand bend.

Ullapool

Torridon

Applecross

Kyle of Lochalsh

Glenelg

Northwest Scotland is big hill country and, for many outdoor enthusiasts, its roads are merely a means to an end – routes to be endured in order to reach the start point for the ascents of the Munros of Torridon, Affric and Kintail. Although many of these roads are beautiful and cycle friendly, not one single mile of the National Cycle Network passes through here. Hands On Events, a Highland events organiser, is more successful in promoting what this part of Scotland can offer the cyclist. Their long-distance sportives bring almost 1000 cyclists to Northwest Scotland every year. In addition to their Ullapool Sportive, the Bealach Mor and Bealach Beag events challenge riders to scale Britain's most feared and revered mountain pass with its 2000ft of climbing. Both sportives approach the Bealach na Ba from the east before dropping down to Applecross in the west. No collection of Highland hillclimbs could justify omitting this giant, but nor can the massive slog up its less lauded western flank be excluded merely for its proximity to what is generally regarded as Britain's top road climb.

It takes routes of this magnitude to overshadow Bealach Ratagan and Bealach na Gaoithe (Torridon) – also two of the toughest climbs in the Highlands. More understated in light of all this drama is the offering above Little Loch Broom at Badrallach, where the single-track road offers unparalleled views of An Teallach, a reminder of the delights for which the region is better known.

NORTHWEST SCOTLAND

BADRALLACH HEIGHTS
LITTLE LOCH BROOM

Distance 2.2 miles/3.6km
Total Height Gain 679ft/207m
Altitude Range 112-774ft/34-236m
Average Gradient 5.8%
Start Roadside boulder at entrance to Badrallach Bothy Croft House (NH 069918)
End Road bend at disused quarry (NH 099916)
Map OS Landranger 19
Rail Garve Station (38 miles)

The 'Great Wilderness' of Fisherfield and Dundonnell contains some of Scotland's remotest high mountains. This little known climb at the end of a road with no through traffic ramps up in the middle and winds down towards the summit before reorienting to face the most celebrated of these peaks – An Teallach.

The remote Badrallach road lies at the end of a seven-mile minor road, branching off the A832. Climb steadily away from the roadside boulder, rising more sharply on approach to the first passing place before easing back in stages through the next two passing places. After the fourth passing place, as the road bends left and a track branches right, you'll encounter the first of several downward dips. It's the ever-changing gradient that makes this climb a more challenging ascent than its statistics suggest.

The right-hand bend at the dip snakes into a left-hand curve, which brings the road to the foot of a long straight. From its high point, there are good views ahead. However, these are soon lost on the undulations that follow. Through a left-hand bend, there's a short stiff climb, easing back

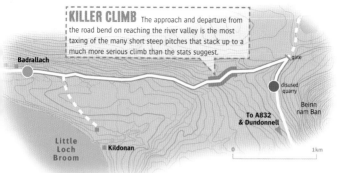

KILLER CLIMB The approach and departure from the road bend on reaching the river valley is the most taxing of the many short steep pitches that stack up to a much more serious climb than the stats suggest.

Badrallach

gate

disused quarry

Beinn nam Ban

To A832 & Dundonnell

Little Loch Broom

Kildonan

0   1km

DISTANCE 2.2 MILES
TOTAL HEIGHT GAIN 679 FEET
AVERAGE GRADIENT 5.8%
CLIMB
PROFILE

at the next passing place, then dipping as the road swings left. Having gained some height from Badrallach, the road now sweeps across the hillside. From the bottom of the dip, it veers away to the right with a sharp return to climbing before straightening up on a long flat section and then dipping down to reach a right-hand bend. The climb picks up from here on a long approach to two left-hand bends that bring about a more marked change in the direction of travel.

At the second left-hand bend, the gradient kicks in with much more force, continuing on the straight and the right-hand bend that follow before finally relenting. The stiff climbing returns halfway along this straight on approach to another

left-hand bend as the road joins and then follows the course of a river valley. It ramps up sharply around the left-hand bend and continues severely on the straight beyond. Your thighs will be screaming out for relief which finally comes in the form of a dip and then a flat section at the right-hand bend at the end. However, you don't get off that lightly – you're in an area famous for such greats as An Teallach, after all – so prepare for the gradient to pick up again, pulling back slightly as it veers to the left at a passing place. Two-thirds of the way along the next straight, the gradient steepens again, relaxing its hold just a little by a distinctive roadside boulder before reaching a false summit.

From here, a short and mercifully gentle climb brings the road to the switchback. Sweeping around to the right, continue ahead for the gradual ascent to the summit, which is reached before the second passing place at a left-hand bend – with An Teallach rising squarely ahead on the horizon.

BEALACH NA GAOITHE
WESTER ALLIGIN, LOCH TORRIDON

Distance 1.6 miles/2.6km
Total Height Gain 781ft/238m
Altitude Range 66-820ft/20-250m
Average Gradient 9.1%
Start Hay pen (NG 844575)
End Parking place on outcrop
(NG 825595)
Map OS Landranger 24
Rail Achnasheen Station (25 miles)

Bealach na Gaoithe, or the The Pass of
the Wind, is a big climb that serves up
challenge after challenge as the road
hauls itself up the gap between Lower
Diabaig and Upper Loch Torridon.

Starting from Wester Alligin, climb
steadily away from the hay pen on the
single-track road, aiming for a right-hand
bend where the climbing begins with a
vengeance. When the road straightens, the
quality improves and a much gentler
gradient follows. This gives way to a steep
switchback to the left which swivels you
round to the road junction, signed as a
path to Inveralligin. Keep left and continue
climbing steeply. There's brief respite
towards the end of the straight before the
incline ramps up around a right-hand bend.
Although the gradient slackens again at the
start of the long straight beyond, what
follows is a steady, gruelling climb past the
static caravan on the left to reach a junction.

Turn left and seize the all-too-brief
opportunity to prepare for what lies above.
The gentle incline gives out after crossing a
cattle grid on approach to a viciously steep
right-hand bend: this gradient now persists
through the straight that follows, passing
the white utility building before a left-hand
bend. The climb eases on the following

To Lower Diabaig

Loch a' Choire Bhig

Bealach na Gaoithe

DISTANCE 1.6 MILES
TOTAL HEIGHT GAIN 781 FEET
AVERAGE GRADIENT 9.1%
CLIMB PROFILE

utility building

cattle grid

To Torridon

Wester Alligin

Upper Loch Torridon

0   500m

straight to a left-hand bend, a pattern that is immediately repeated. The gradient eases at the higher bend and the direction of travel changes. A gently sweeping Z-bend brings a small waterfall into view, but briefly, as the road drifts up to the foot of the final assault on the bealach.

From here, the road climbs ever more stiffly on a short straight and around a right-hand bend before softening slightly on the straight leading to a right switchback turn. The climbing intensifies after the turn, easing back momentarily at a passing place, but then steepening to pass the viewpoint to the right.

Be warned, the dip beyond the viewpoint signifies only a break in the ascent and not an end to the torture. The road swoops straight down and then to the right before an abrupt return to stiff climbing at a left-hand bend under telegraph poles. The gradient finally eases as the road winds through the narrow bealach. There are two

false summits, one after a short steep pitch, the other at the line of snow poles after a gentle sweep around the lochan. A short but severe downhill is followed by an even steeper pitch that will have you gasping for air as you aim for the road's highest point at the second line of snow poles on the rocky outcrop. The outstanding views of Loch Diabaigas Airde, not to mention the sense of achievement that comes from bagging one of the country's top road summits, may just be enough tempt you back again – but maybe not for a while!

BEALACH NA BA (WEST)
APPLECROSS

Distance 5.5 miles/8.9km
Total Height Gain 2014ft/614m
Altitude Range 23-2037ft/7-621m
Average Gradient 6.9%
Start Road junction (NG 713446)
End Passing place beyond road/track junction (NG 775425)
Map OS Landranger 24
Rail Strathcarron Station (22 miles)

More typically enjoyed as a descent, there are more than 2000 good reasons to tackle this giant if you like your conquests hard won. If the gods are with you, you'll also have the benefit of the wind at your back.

Climb steeply away from the junction on a wide twin track road of excellent quality that contradicts the warning signs. An S-bend (left, then sweeping right) leads into a left-hand switchback. The short straight that follows ends at a 90° right-hand bend, and on the next straight the road narrows to single track and the gradient drops a few notches. Towards the right-hand bend after a cattle grid, the gradient picks up again, crossing a burn before aiming northeast through ferns and rough grassland to the edge of a plantation.

Here, the forest to the left and hillside to the right afford shelter and the incline is gentle. Four right-hand bends reorient the road, still protected from the elements, to cross a stone bridge as the forest is finally

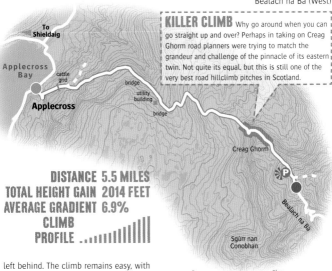

DISTANCE 5.5 MILES
TOTAL HEIGHT GAIN 2014 FEET
AVERAGE GRADIENT 6.9%
CLIMB
PROFILE

left behind. The climb remains easy, with some undulations, as the course of the Allt Beag is followed. Soon after a corrugated iron building, a left-hand bend leads to another stone bridge – marking the start of a stiff section of ascent.

After a relentlessly rising straight comes a right-hand bend, swiftly followed by a left-hand bend and another long straight. A sweeping curve to the right changes the direction of travel towards the steep face of a rocky outcrop. A series of left-hand bends carry the road around the exposed rock, where it levels out before a right-hand bend.

What follows is a procession of undulating straights with an upward trajectory, which cut through bogland on approach to the cliff face – the ultimate challenge this side of the bealach. The road steepens towards the end of the last of these straights, where two

right-hand bends preclude you from having to make a direct ascent, and a switchback to the left continues this good fortune. The pitch appears to top out after a sharp right-hand bend at the end of the next straight, but there's no need for jubilation yet – it's a false summit.

From here, the road continues to rise steeply towards the summit transmitter, now clearly in view, with the gradient only eventually pulling back at a marked right-hand bend. The incline eases further at the left-hand bend beyond, and the remainder of the route is a steady climb, weaving around rocky outcrops to take the route of least resistance: the end is the passing place after the transmitter track junction.

BEALACH NA BA (EAST)
LOCH KISHORN

Distance 5.25 miles/8.4km
Total Height Gain 2028ft/618m
Altitude Range 10-2037ft/3-621m
Average Gradient 7.3%
Start The lochside (NG 829413)
End Passing place before road/track junction (NG 775425)
Map OS Landranger 24
Rail Strathcarron Station (10 miles)

Sportives serve up the Bealach na Ba in a 90-mile package in the autumn and a 43-mile package in the spring, but the 2000ft climb is a gargantuan challenge in its own right.

The route starts with an abrupt ascent from the lochside on the road to Kishorn. Pass through the gates near the top to reach a junction, where you turn left. It's an act of bare-faced deceit that this route should have such an unremarkable beginning as the road rises steadily up a fairly featureless hillside, an initial straight leading to a left-hand bend. A series of shorter straights follow, with a marked change of direction after the second right-hand bend. Aiming for the bulk of Sgurr a' Chaorachain, another long straight gives way to a series of shorter straights, with two right-hand bends reorienting the direction of travel.

A long sweep now follows, initially turning away from the Sgurr to tackle the slopes more directly by a burn, swinging left to cross this and then traverse the hillside. The road levels at the start of a

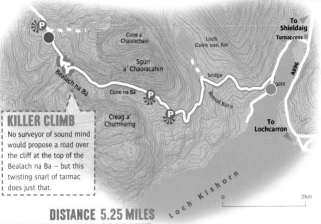

Coire a'
Chaorachain

Loch
Coire nan Arr

Sgùrr
a' Chaoracahin

bridge

gate

A896

Coire na Ba

Russell Burn

Bealach na Ba

Creag a'
Chumhaing

To
Lochcarron

KILLER CLIMB

No surveyor of sound mind
would propose a road over
the cliff at the top of the
Bealach na Ba – but this
twisting snarl of tarmac
does just that.

Loch Kishorn

0   2km

DISTANCE 5.25 MILES
TOTAL HEIGHT GAIN 2028 FEET
AVERAGE GRADIENT 7.3%
CLIMB
PROFILE ....||||||||

straight headed back towards the Sgurr,
carrying on over the stone bridge across
the Russell Burn.

By the track junction at the end of the
straight, a 90° turn marks a return to
climbing with a series of right-hand bends
as the road works its way around the spur.
After a more marked right-hand bend and
then a left-hand bend, the road steepens
even more to gain the crest of the spur,
with crash barriers indicating the severity
of the incline on the downslope.

A wide sweep around the crest brings
the Bealach na Ba into view, the road then
aiming back towards the Sgurr before
reorienting itself towards Creag a'
Chumhaing by a pair of left-hand bends.

A sweeping right-hand bend brings the
Bealach back into full view.

What follows is a long and taxing climb
on the Coire na Ba, with good forward
vision throughout and plenty of passing
places. As the road passes above and
beyond the waterfall, it swings left to begin
the final approach to the Bealach na Ba.
Crash barriers provide a degree of comfort!

The final push is as exhilarating as it is
excruciating. Three switchbacks and five
bends divide the straights that carry the
road up to round a summit knoll with a Z-
bend. It would seem an ideal end point for
Britain's ultimate hillclimb challenge, but
the summit lies further ahead. Initially, the
road levels out on a straight to pass a
lochan on the right, before cranking up with
a series of right-hand bends to negotiate,
and finally topping out at the passing place
before the transmitter track turn-off.

BEALACH RATAGAN LOCH DUICH

Distance 2.6 miles/4.1km
Total Height Gain 1099ft/335m
Altitude Range 13-1112ft/4-339m
Average Gradient 8.2%
Start Picnic place (NG 926190)
End Road bend (NG 903198)
Map OS Landranger 33
Rail Kyle of Lochalsh Station (16 miles)

An insanely steep ramp ratchets up the difficulty of an already tough climb which, after an initial warm-up away from Loch Duich, becomes an unrelenting slog.

Climb stiffly away from the lochside picnic area, weaving up to reach a junction. Turn right to join a single-track road towards Glenelg and grab this brief opportunity to prepare for what lies ahead as the forest encroaches on all sides and the gradient eases. Occasional breaks in the cover afford views down to Ratagan and across Loch Duich. Although the climb is not taxing and there is reasonable forward vision, the grass banking on the downside prevents cars from moving aside for ascending cyclists and if descending vehicles overshoot the passing places some tight squeezes must be negotiated.

The gentler climbing gives out in stages – at the stone wall to the right, the track junction to the left and after the second bridge that sits aside its stone predecessor. It is perhaps best not to dwell on the fact that there is now no significant easing of gradient until the summit viewpoint. Thankfully, the shorter bends of the lower climb give way to longer straights and the

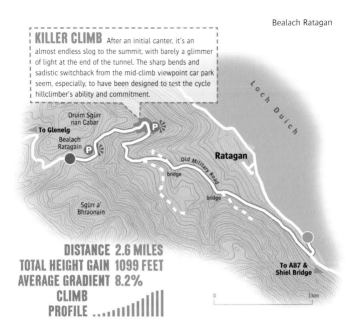

KILLER CLIMB After an initial canter, it's an almost endless slog to the summit, with barely a glimmer of light at the end of the tunnel. The sharp bends and sadistic switchback from the mid-climb viewpoint car park seem, especially, to have been designed to test the cycle hillclimber's ability and commitment.

DISTANCE 2.6 MILES
TOTAL HEIGHT GAIN 1099 FEET
AVERAGE GRADIENT 8.2%
CLIMB
PROFILE

road alternates between wide twin-track and single track, leaving the earlier bypassing hazards behind.

After almost 1.4 miles of tough climbing (covering 560ft at an average gradient of 7%), the sign warning of a steeper climb ahead will make you want to weep. The road sweeps right and rises more directly up the hillside. At the end of this straight, it kinks left and then makes a sharper left to pass a viewpoint car park to the right. The views below make this well worth a stop, although the thought of starting up again may quash any such temptation.

Beyond the car park, the difficulty of the climb intensifies, particularly at the

switchback to the left. The road continues to rise stiffly as it straightens, relenting only as it veers right at the crash barriers.

From here to the summit, it's a steady grind on longer straights with gentle bends and a more open aspect as height is gained. The tough climbing ends on rounding the left-hand bend at the higher viewpoint car park. A short level straight means you can enjoy the views without dismounting this time – that may be the better choice as the summit of the climb is still a little further on. Turn sharp right away from the viewpoint to climb: the road tops out at the first passing place above the treeline on the left.

63

HARRIS

3

NORTH
UIST

2

Portree ●

1

SOUTH
UIST

SKYE

homage to one man's gargantuan
achievement on Calum's Road and look back
at the imposing peaks of the Black Cuillin on
the journey over is just too good to miss out.

With a reputation for hardcore climbs and
scrambles that comes form having such a
world-renowned mountain range, Skye has
its fair share of challenges for the road
cyclist, too, and to pick off the best of these
is no easy task. Here, the energy-sapping
approach to the Quiraing is made more than
worthwhile by the drama of the final climb
up the Trotternish escarpment.

BARRA

4

For most visitors the
Skye Bridge is the first
introduction to the largest
and most northerly of the islands
in the Inner Hebrides, but those
seeking that island sensation on arrival can
still take the tourist ferry to Skye in the
summer months, disembarking at Kylerhea
to be confronted by the 915ft climb up to
the Bealach Udal, en route to the heart of
Skye. In truth, nothing quite matches that
feeling of ambling off a Hebridean ferry with
all the anticipation of treasures ahead, and
the Isle of Raasay, reached via ferry from
Sconser on Skye, allows you to do just that.
For the road cyclist, the chance both to pay

Not all Hebridean islands are well
endowed with hillclimb challenges, but on
Harris, the short climb up from Reinigeadal
is a hidden gem.

Rounding off this collection is the climb
away from Castlebay on Barra, another short
ascent where the views down towards the
town and across to the smaller islands at
the southern end of the Outer Hebrides
island chain are incomparable.

THE HEBRIDES

CALUM'S ROAD ISLE OF RAASAY

Distance North: 0.9 miles/1.4km.
South: 0.55 miles/0.9km

Total Height Gain North: 358ft/109m.
South: 190ft/58m

Altitude Range North: 59-344ft/18-105m.
South: 194-344ft/59-105m

Average Gradient North: 7.7%. South: 6.6%

Start North: Road/track junction, bay, west
of Arnish (NG 591479). South: Road/track
junction, Brochel (NG 583464)

End North: Passing place at exposed rock
outcrop (NG 591474). South: Passing place
before North end point (NG 591474)

Map OS Landranger 24

Ferry Raasay Ferry Terminal (9 miles)

Calum MacLeod (1911–1988) was a
crofter, postman and lighthouse keeper
who famously built the stretch of road
between Brochel Castle and Arnish over a
period of 10 years, using crude tools and
sheer persistence after years of conflict
between local residents and the council
over the lack of road access. Although
this inspiring legacy is the main driver
for visiting, these climbs from the coast
to the rock-strewn moor are also tough
challenges in a dramatic setting.

North: Grit your teeth for a sharp ramp
from the dip, cresting at the passing place
before easing left around the headland of
Rubha Crion. The road continues to rise
steeply on the straight beyond, cresting again
at the passing place after the sign warning of
falling boulders. Now following the line of the
rockface, respite comes in a steep descent, a
gentle climb and a drop to a 90° bend.

The sharp climb away from the bend
intensifies as the road veers left round an
outcrop. With the coast at your back, this
pitch tops out after the large passing place,
then drops once more. From the right-hand
bend that follows lies a steep pitch up to an
exposed crag. The gradient then slackens on
approach to a wide switchback to the right,
which appears as if from nowhere. The
summit is reached by way of a long straight
– convex in profile but steep throughout

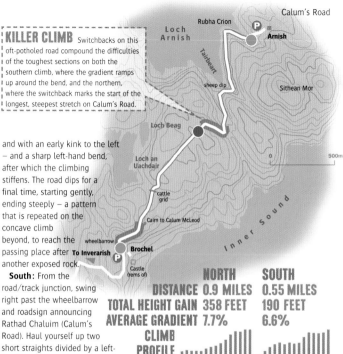

KILLER CLIMB Switchbacks on this oft-potholed road compound the difficulties of the toughest sections on both the southern climb, where the gradient ramps up around the bend, and the northern, where the switchback marks the start of the longest, steepest stretch on Calum's Road.

and with an early kink to the left – and a sharp left-hand bend, after which the climbing stiffens. The road dips for a final time, starting gently, ending steeply – a pattern that is repeated on the concave climb beyond, to reach the passing place after **To Inverarish** another exposed rock.

South: From the road/track junction, swing right past the wheelbarrow and roadsign announcing Rathad Chaluim (Calum's Road). Haul yourself up two short straights divided by a left-hand bend to reach a passing place at a false summit. A quick dip and a steeper step-up around another left-hand bend brings into view the memorial cairn to Calum Macleod, reached by way of a gentle incline – if you find riding this route hard-going, imagine what extraordinary energy and dedication it took to build it.

A brief dip, then a gently rising straight is followed by a short steep ramp up to a passing place. After a gentle dip to a cattle grid, road quality improves but the climbing resumes as the road sweeps to the right,

	NORTH	SOUTH
DISTANCE	0.9 MILES	0.55 MILES
TOTAL HEIGHT GAIN	358 FEET	190 FEET
AVERAGE GRADIENT	7.7%	6.6%
CLIMB PROFILE		

the gradient kicking in viciously on the sharp left-hand bend at the end of the straight. There's a staged decrease in the incline to reach a lower summit at the passing place, where a gradual descent now cuts through a flat expanse of heather. The roadsign warning of a flying pig over road humps should be heeded, if only on account of the severe bump that lies ahead.

The summit lies at the top of a short, steep ramp, beyond a left-hand bend at the end of the lumpy straight.

QUIRAING STAFFIN, ISLE OF SKYE

Distance 2.5 miles/4km
Total Height Gain 794ft/242m
Altitude Range 66-853ft/20-260m
Average Gradient 6.1%
Start Bridge over River Brogaig
(NG 471679)
End Road bend at car park (NG 437677)
Map OS Landranger 23
Rail Kyle of Lochalsh Station (51 miles)

**A long preamble to the foot of the
Trotternish Ridge is followed by an
abrupt ascent, ending on an
unbelievably steep hairpin bend.**

This route starts gently on the straight,
with the incline kicking in at the first left-
hand bend. This stiffer gradient continues
around a right-hand bend, leading up to the
Quiraing road junction where you turn left.

After the road becomes single track, there
starts a long transitional section of gentler
climbing through pastures and rough
grasses, all the while in the shadow of the
towering ridges and dramatic rock
formations of the Trotternish Ridge.

Sweeping bends and long straights carry
the road up to the junction to Sartle, with
its improbable lone petrol pump. The steady
climbing resumes through a Z-bend away
from the junction.

Two right-hand bends punctuate the
straights as the road skirts the foot of an
embankment and passes above a cemetery.
From the second bend, the route aims for
the foot of the hill on which Dun Beag fort
sits. Following a left-hand bend, the road
skirts the edge of this hillside to another
left-hand bend, which carries it over a burn.

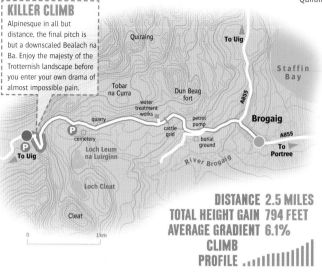

KILLER CLIMB

Alpinesque in all but distance, the final pitch is but a downscaled Bealach na Ba. Enjoy the majesty of the Trotternish landscape before you enter your own drama of almost impossible pain.

DISTANCE 2.5 MILES
TOTAL HEIGHT GAIN 794 FEET
AVERAGE GRADIENT 6.1%
CLIMB
PROFILE

Now aiming for Cleat, the climb steepens. After crossing a cattle grid and rough, rutted dip, and passing the entrance to the Staffin Water Treatment Works, a wide sweeping bend to the right brings the Trotternish Ridge into full view. The road rises very gently, passing through some equally soft bends, before it drops down and flattens out along the edge of the banking at the bottom of Tobar na Curra.

The incline picks up slightly at the right-hand bend beyond the old quarry as it leaves the straight behind. Beyond the cemetery to the left, the road steepens further as a Z-bend carries it around a knoll. Two straights broken by a left-hand bend bring the road to the foot of the long approach to the summit.

Another left-hand bend reorients the road to rise steadily and steeply up and across the hillside, with further left-hand bends keeping the gradient manageable.

The final stage is Alpinesque in setting and severity – if not in distance. On reaching the crash barriers over the burn, the single-track road veers to the left. Viewed from here, the upper reaches of the climb seem totally beyond reach – that the summit is attainable at all is down to the steepening stretch of road from the switchback and a sting-in-the-tail at the end of the straight beyond. As the road widens, there is a bend to the right, then an excruciatingly steep second hairpin bend to the left. Beyond this, the steep pitch continues up to the summit car park.

69

LOCH BEAG, REINIGEADAL
ISLE OF HARRIS

Distance 1.2 miles/1.9km
Total Height Gain 525ft/160m
Altitude Range 33-558ft/10-170m
Average Gradient 8.6%
Start Road/track junction beyond postbox (NB 227018)
End Sheep pen above Loch Beag (NB 220028)
Map OS Landranger 14
Ferry Tarbert Ferry Terminal (12 miles)

Two steep ramps of 13% are squeezed into the preliminary stages of the toughest climb in the Outer Hebrides.

Climb away from Reinigeadal with the immediate goal of reaching the highest point above this settlement by way of a 13% climb. The gradient kicks in around a right-hand bend, with crash barriers offering protection on the climbing side. The short straight beyond soon blends into a wide sweeping switchback to the left, slicing through an impressively deep cleft at the bend before stiffening some more and then continuing steeply up the exit straight. Beyond the utility building, views down to the lochside confirm what your screaming legs are suggesting – much height has been gained, although few metres carried forward.

A right-hand bend takes the road up to the lower cattle grid, and the incline eases. A further slackening of the gradient midway along the straight carries the road gently to the bottom of another right-hand bend, which starts where the footpath to Tarbert leaves the road to the left. Along this straight, it is worth soaking up the views of Loch Trolamaraig and the slopes that tumble steeply to its shores.

There is now a return to climbing at a 13% gradient. The road narrows around the

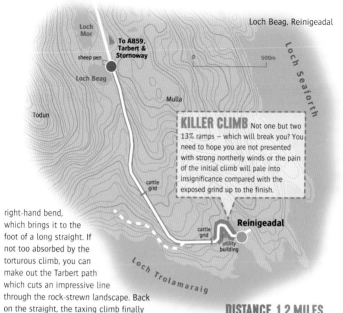

Loch Beag, Reinigeadal

KILLER CLIMB Not one but two 13% ramps – which will break you? You need to hope you are not presented with strong northerly winds or the pain of the initial climb will pale into insignificance compared with the exposed grind up to the finish.

right-hand bend, which brings it to the foot of a long straight. If not too absorbed by the torturous climb, you can make out the Tarbert path which cuts an impressive line through the rock-strewn landscape. Back on the straight, the taxing climb finally crests a short way after another cattle grid. The straight now carries forward more gently, with the grey peak of Todun dominating the view throughout.

The right-hand bend at the end of the straight marks a return to steeper climbing. Views open up ahead, giving refreshing glimpses of the waterfall that cascades down the upper reaches of the Abhainn Loteger and more ominous warnings of the concave slope that must be scaled to reach the summit of this climb. The gradient remains steady on the long approach, which comprises two straights separated by a left-hand bend. On reaching the passing place to the left, the climb ramps up for a final time, veering to the right to enter a cutting.

DISTANCE 1.2 MILES
TOTAL HEIGHT GAIN 525 FEET
AVERAGE GRADIENT 8.6%
CLIMB PROFILE ..mmlllllll

From below, it appears that the upper end of this will be the finish line for the climb. However, the stiff ascent relents at the passing place beyond the cutting and eases back in stages to reach the summit proper at the passing place by the sheep pen above Loch Beag. Although the road carries on up to a high point above Lochan an Fheoir, few extra metres are gained in height over more than a mile of undulating road.

CASTLEBAY ISLE OF BARRA

Distance 0.7 miles/1.1km
Total Height Gain 321ft/98m
Altitude Range 13-335ft/4-102m
Average Gradient 8.7%
Start Fence/road junction on A888
(NL 671982)
End Solar-powered mast (NL 680987)
Map OS Landranger 31
Ferry Castlebay Ferry Terminal (<1 mile)

The highest point on the Barra ring road can be gained in little more than one mile from the ferry terminal.

This climb is beset by false starts as the A888 heads east away from Castlebay,
rearing up only to dip back down again twice. It is better to consider the start of the climb to be half a mile from the ferry terminal, near the foot of the long straight to the east of the village where the fence and the burn join it on the left.

The gentle climb from here to a white cottage follows a mostly single-track road which is in excellent condition throughout. The difficulty cranks up in three gradual stages along the straight – at the cottage, at the left-hand bend beyond the junction for Garrygall and, most significantly, after the turn-off for An Gleann (the Glen) to the left. From here, all that is

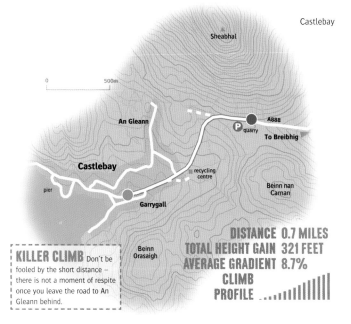

KILLER CLIMB Don't be fooled by the short distance – there is not a moment of respite once you leave the road to An Gleann behind.

DISTANCE 0.7 MILES
TOTAL HEIGHT GAIN 321 FEET
AVERAGE GRADIENT 8.7%
CLIMB PROFILE ....ııillllll

left to do is grind relentlessly up to the summit.

Beyond the Garrygall recycling centre, another left-hand bend orients the road towards the shoulder of Sheabhal (383m), between its highest point and the distinctive white marble statue of the Madonna and Child. A kink to the left at a track junction is followed by another short straight that carries the road up to a right-hand sweep as the summit is approached.

Stiff climbing continues on the short straight beyond, soon topping out at the solar-powered mast that overlooks the shallow quarry to the right.

From here, you have a few options,

depending on how shaky your legs are at this point. You can leave the bike behind for a rough scramble up the rock-strewn hillside to the summit of Sheabhal and its spectacular views over the bay, or carry on to complete the 13-mile cycle around the island. Alternatively, just drop down to ascend the much rougher eastern side of this climb (one mile in distance from sea level away from Breibhig). If that sounds like too much effort, turn around, take in the views and then whizz back down to Castlebay, no doubt acknowledging motorists who tend to pull over in the passing places to let you make the most of the descent!

FORT WILLIAM

1

3 Strontian

Glencoe

2

Tobermory

MULL

4

Lochaber markets itself as the outdoor capital of the UK, with Fort William as its centrepiece. Located at the foot of Ben Nevis, the UK's highest mountain, at the northern end of the West Highland Way, Scotland's premier long-distance walking trail, at the southern end of the Caledonian Canal, and just a few miles from the Nevis Range Mountain Resort, it is no surprise that Fort William is a Mecca for hill, snow and water sports enthusiasts. For cyclists, meanwhile, emotions in Fort William may swing from the adrenalin rush of the annual UCI Mountain Bike World Cup downhill event to respectful reverence at the Ghost bike at Carrs Corner, which marks the spot where Jason MacIntyre, one of Scotland's most promising talents, lost his life in a road accident in 2008.

With so much competition from the hillwalking, mountaineering and downhilling worlds, road hillclimbing is not the first sport with which Fort William is associated. However, one tough climb, Lundavra Road, may yet earn its place in the area's canon of more famous outdoor challenges.

A challenge of an entirely different nature awaits a few miles south at Glencoe, where the 15-mile slog up to Rannoch Moor carries the rider through one of Scotland's most spectacular glens.

South of Lochaber, on Mull, the short, sharp shock of a climb through Glen Leidle more than justifies the effort required to reach this remote island outpost.

Mouth-watering as these are, though, nothing quite tops the western ascent of the Bealach Feith nan Laogh. With an average 11.9% gradient over an unforgiving 1.6 miles, this is a strong contender for the title of Scotland's toughest climb.

SOUTH OF FORT WILLIAM

LUNDAVRA ROAD FORT WILLIAM

Distance 1 mile/1.6km
Total Height Gain 469ft/143m
Altitude Range 20-486ft/6-148m
Average Gradient 8.9%
Start Roundabout (NN 099736)
End Car park (NN 097721)
Map OS Landranger 41
Rail Fort William Station (<1 mile)

Though mercifully short, you'll still need heaps of energy to rise to the challenge of this one-mile ascent above Fort William.

Leave the A82 at the southern end of the High Street to climb steeply away from the roundabout, headed in the direction of Upper Achintore. The incline persists around the right-hand bend beyond the West End Hotel car park, after which a steep straight hauls the road up to the junction with Union Road at a left-hand bend. Respite only comes in the form of a less severe climb – and it is brief – as the gradient picks up from Argyll Terrace, steepening further towards the end of the straight on approach to a second left-hand bend.

Now Lundavra Road leaves nothing to the imagination, as ahead lies a long straight with a lot of climbing to negotiate. Grand views down to Loch Linnhe on the right may raise the spirits or at least distract from what follows. The straight comprises three sharp climbs, each interspersed with a short section of less severe climbing. The first is a concave pitch, with the incline kicking in between the first bus stop and the Connochie Road junction on the left. The second and shortest pitch starts at the roadside steps to the left, and rises steeply up to the point at which the wall ends on the right. The third pitch is a long haul from

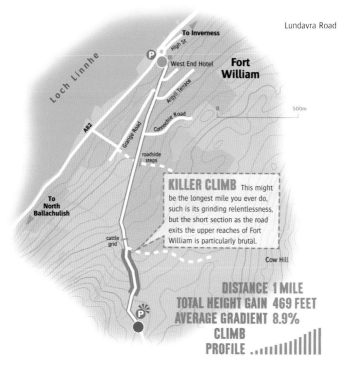

To Inverness

Fort William

West End Hotel

High St.

Argyll Terrace

Connochie Road

Loch Linnhe

A82

Grange Road

roadside steps

To North Ballachulish

cattle grid

KILLER CLIMB This might be the longest mile you ever do, such is its grinding relentlessness, but the short section as the road exits the upper reaches of Fort William is particularly brutal.

Cow Hill

0   500m

DISTANCE 1 MILE
TOTAL HEIGHT GAIN 469 FEET
AVERAGE GRADIENT 8.9%
CLIMB PROFILE IIIIIIII

Caithness Place and Loch Linnhe Lodge to the left-hand bend at the end of the straight.

More pain is to come as Lundavra Road steepens further around it, but straightens on approach to and beyond the cattle grid with gentler climbing as the last houses of upper Fort William are left behind and the road heads up towards open countryside.

The challenge ramps up after the road passes the track to the Cow Hill transmitter on the left. The road veers to the left and remains just as steep as it straightens, easing only briefly before the stiff climbing

resumes to gain a false summit on a right-hand bend between two passing places on the left. Your recovery time at the higher passing place is woefully short as the stiff incline is soon back to test you again. The sweeping views beyond Cow Hill towards Ben Nevis make the climb worth the effort, though there is little chance to truly enjoy them until the job is done. The gradient slackens on reaching a right-hand bend, before the road crosses a small burn. Finally swinging to the right, then left, the climb tops out at the Blarmachfoldach viewpoint.

GLENCOE AND RANNOCH MOOR

Distance 15.1 miles/24.2km
Total Height Gain 1378ft/420m
Altitude Range 13-1124ft/4-343m
Average Gradient 1.7%
Start Road junction, A82/B863
(NN 097587)
End Summit road sign (NN 304515)
Map OS Landranger 41
Rail Fort William Station (10 miles)

A long but exhilarating climb rising 1000ft through one of Scotland's most atmospheric and iconic glens to the edge of the bleak expanse of Rannoch Moor.

The long haul to the road summit of Rannoch Moor starts with a comfortable climb on a series of long straights divided by gentle bends. The first straight ends with a sweeping bend to the right and is followed by three further long straights heading southeast, before turning more markedly to the left to bear east.

Another long straight lies around the bend. The road veers to the left at the end of this straight and the incline steepens on approach to the junction with the minor road on the left that peels back towards Glencoe village. Beyond the junction, the

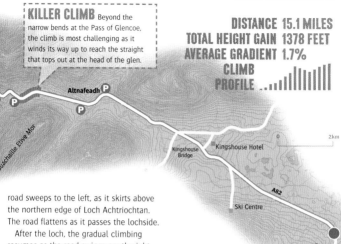

KILLER CLIMB Beyond the narrow bends at the Pass of Glencoe, the climb is most challenging as it winds its way up to reach the straight that tops out at the head of the glen.

DISTANCE 15.1 MILES
TOTAL HEIGHT GAIN 1378 FEET
AVERAGE GRADIENT 1.7%
CLIMB PROFILE

Altnafeadh

Buachaille Etive Mor

Kingshouse Bridge

Kingshouse Hotel

2km

A82

Ski Centre

To Tyndrum

road sweeps to the left, as it skirts above the northern edge of Loch Achtriochtan. The road flattens as it passes the lochside.

After the loch, the gradual climbing resumes as the road swings gently right, hugging the northern side of Glen Coe. The River Coe lies on the other side, across a wide and flat valley floor. There is a brief dip after the stone bridge at the track junction leading to the isolated steading of Achtriochtan.

From here, the climbing stiffens and the valley narrows. Initially, the straights continue, although after the second of two parking places/viewpoints on the right, the road veers sharply right and begins a section of much shorter straights, interspersed with sharper bends. The road is also narrower and traffic is likely to pose as much of a challenge as the climb. Further on, the incline stiffens more, this steeper incline easing at the milestone near the start of the straight that lies beyond the right-hand bend. The initial climb tops out beyond the parking place on the right and

just as the road curves away to the left.

The sweep to the left marks the start of a transition section of descent and flats. This drop continues around the wide sweeping bend to the right at Altnafeadh and ends on the straight beyond. A flat section is followed by a further descent, with a trio of gentle bends (right, left, right) bringing the road to a straight that leads down to the distinctive Kingshouse Bridge.

The final climb to the road summit on Rannoch Moor starts from the bridge, initially through short straights divided by wide, sweeping bends. Two long straights follow, together over 4km in length. Shortly beyond the right-hand bend at the end of the second straight, a road sign marks the summit at 1124ft.

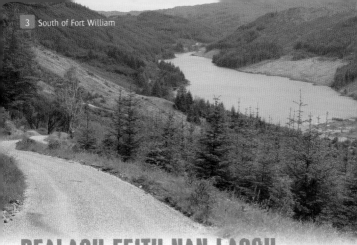

BEALACH FEITH NAN LAOGH
LOCH DOILET, NORTH OF STRONTIAN

Distance 1.6 miles/2.6km
Total Height Gain 1027ft/313m
Altitude Range 98-1125ft/30-343m
Average Gradient 11.9%
Start Road/track junction (NM 818673)
End Road bend (NM 837665)
Map OS Landranger 40
Rail Fort William Station (27 miles)

Bealach Feith nan Laogh, or The Pass of the Bog and Calf, presents the very worst and the very best of hillclimb road quality in Scotland in a single gargantuan challenge.

The climb to the bealach is severe from the outset as the road pulls away from the track junction to Kinlochan. A short straight soon gives way to a right-hand bend that in turn sweeps into a right-hand switchback.

A longer straight after the switchback ends with the first of four sharp bends, each followed by a very short straight as the road worms its way up to reach a left-hand switchback to cross the Allt Druim Sliabhain. Road quality has been poor to this point. From here, resurfacing transforms the climbing experience.

What follows is one of Scotland's toughest 2km of road climbing. Although the direction of travel is fairly constant and forward vision is better than you might expect from a forest road, blind summits and small bends ensure that the climber never has to confront the full magnitude of what lies ahead. The granny gear is likely to be spinning and the heart rate will be approaching max throughout.

As a result of tree felling on the

80

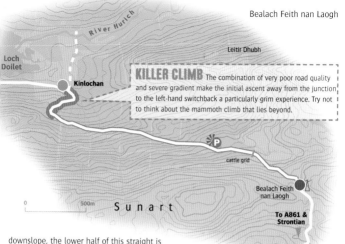

KILLER CLIMB The combination of very poor road quality and severe gradient make the initial ascent away from the junction to the left-hand switchback a particularly grim experience. Try not to think about the mammoth climb that lies beyond.

Loch Doilet

River Hurich

Leitir Dhubh

Kinlochan

cattle grid

Bealach Feith nan Laogh

To A861 & Strontian

0 — 500m

S u n a r t

downslope, the lower half of this straight is visible from the outset. However, this is soon lost as the incline kicks in and the road negotiates a series of very tight bends, which also makes it more difficult to gain climbing momentum. The straights lengthen between the second and third river crossings (marked by striped bollards on either side of the road). After the final crossing, the road rises in stepped stages to enter the gloom of mature forest.

With more tree cover, expect more natural debris on the road. The gradient steepens at the second passing place, then pulls back at the next left-hand bend. Ramping up again as the road picks up crash barriers on the downslope, the incline then weakens in two stages as it reaches the forest parking area for the Loch Doilet viewpoint. A sweeping bend around the parking area is followed by a straight, a right-hand bend and then a more gentle ascent to the forest edge.

DISTANCE 1.6 MILES
TOTAL HEIGHT GAIN 1027 FEET
AVERAGE GRADIENT 11.9%
CLIMB
PROFILE IIIIII

A cattle grid marks the start of more open moorland. On approach, both the landscape and the easing gradient give the impression that the climb crests at the right-hand bend beyond. The illusion is soon shattered. A long stiff climb on a straight leads up to a left-hand bend and a further short straight that approaches the sting-in-the-tail. On a final series of tight bends, the difficulty cranks up as the road picks up crash barriers, continuing stiffly on the straight after it leaves them behind. The climb tops out abruptly at the left-hand bend adjacent to the mast.

GLEN LEIDLE CARSAIG, THE ISLE OF MULL

Distance 1.5 miles/2.5km
Total Height Gain 659ft/201m
Altitude Range 36-614ft/11-187m
Average Gradient 8.1%
Start Pier at end of Glen Leidle road, off A849 at Pennyghael (NM 544213)
End Road bend (NM 533232)
Map OS Landranger 48
Rail Craignure Ferry Terminal (23 miles)

A remarkably diverse climb crammed in to little more than a mile in a far-flung corner of the island on the Ross of Mull.

Climb steeply away from the road end to reach a false summit. Easing back to sweep around a gentle Z-bend, the incline steepens as the straight is regained and then again as the road picks up crash barriers on the downslope. The grinding climb persists as it swings sharply at 90° to the right. A few more degrees of ascent are eked out beyond Power House, the roadside villa. This pitch continues up to the lower entrance to Inniemore Lodge, finally easing back on reaching its oversized 'shed' at the upper entrance.

Respite follows. A curve to the left is taken on the level and is followed by a gentle descent on the straight, with views opening up towards the Aird Ghlas cliffs on the other side of Carsaig Bay. On re-entering forest, after three gentle bends, the descent steepens, and the road sweeps down to the right to reach the bridge crossing the foot of a dramatic waterfall. Marvel also at the oddly-sited telephone box.

The return to climbing is gradual at first, as the road negotiates gentle bends away from the bridge to start curving its way up and across the wooded hillside. A more marked S-bend takes the road over the first of four stone bridges. The incline steepens

DISTANCE 1.5 MILES
TOTAL HEIGHT GAIN 659 FEET
AVERAGE GRADIENT 8.1%
CLIMB PROFILE

KILLER CLIMB

The pitch around Power House is sure to drain your energy levels.

on passing the second stone bridge, easing back beyond the third at a right-hand bend. This levelling off is followed by a return to steady climbing after a left-hand bend.

On approach to the final bridge in the forest, at the edge of the moor, the climb ramps up. The road swings right, with the protection of crash barriers to the left, with views beginning to open up on the straight ahead to the waterfall falling from the side of Cnoc a' Bhraghad. A right-hand bend is followed by another straight and a clearer vision of what lies ahead as the road grinds its way up to a narrow gap, with only a

momentary relaxing of the gradient as it crosses a stone bridge on the way.

Aspect opens up to the right as the road steepens further to enter the gap. The incline slackens at the second telegraph pole, after which the climbing is stiff rather than severe. An S-bend is followed by a straight with a gentler climb to the foot of the knoll. A left-hand bend reorients the road and there is one last blast of stiff climbing on the final straight. The false summit at its end is compensated for by the views ahead to Ben More and the knowledge that the summit lies just a few metres away.

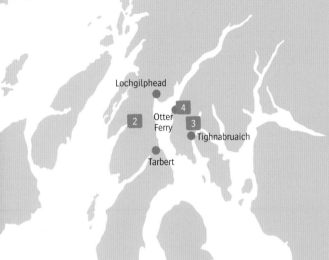

Lochgilphead

4

2 Otter
Ferry

3

Tighnabruaich

Tarbert

Campbeltown

1

Argyll is a cycling paradise with scenic roads and less of the heavy traffic that characterises the more accessible countryside around Scotland's larger towns and cities. Its remoteness means that this area tends only to be enjoyed as part of longer cycle tours. Indeed, some of the best that the region has to offer is very far removed from the humdrum of urban life.

The hidden jewel in Argyll's crown is without question the Mull of Kintyre. The headland is immortalised in song, but the road to its lighthouse remains one of Scottish cycling's best-kept secrets, while further up the peninsula, the road up Knapdale is one of the few hillclimbs to be found here.

Not all of Argyll's roads are remote or without renown. The Kyles of Bute are spectacular from the viewpoint above the sea lochs of the Clyde, and this makes a great objective for an ascent from Tighnabruaich. Also in the more accessible reaches of Argyll is the climb up the heavily forested hill road from Glendaruel to Bealach Maim en route to Otter Ferry.

ARGYLL

MULL OF KINTYRE

Distance 1.4 miles/2.2km
Total Height Gain 981ft/299m
Altitude Range 279-1,224ft/85-373m
Average Gradient 13.6%
Start Mull of Kintyre lighthouse
(NR 588085)
End Road/track junction (NR 601081)
Map OS Landranger 68
Rail Oban (96 miles)

Arguably the ultimate hillclimb challenge in Southern Scotland, which starts with a descent down to the Mull of Kintyre lighthouse. Comprising a climb of almost 1000ft in less than one and a half miles, it is spectacular in its severity.

Road quality is rough throughout and vigilance will be required to avoid loose stones and large potholes. The route starts with a characteristically steep ascent away from the lighthouse, sweeping to the right past the lower radio transmitter (enclosed within a high barbed wire fence on the right). At the end of the straight that follows, the road turns sharply left, passing between the heliport and septic tanks and upper radio transmitter. Although remaining steep, the gradient lessens on passing through a gap in the wall, only to stiffen at a wide switchback to the right. This changes the direction of travel and leads to another straight, at the end of which the road bends left and heads up towards the ruined farmhouse of Ballinamoill.

The straight that lies beyond the sharp switchback to the left above Ballinamoill brings the road to the foot of a set of three steep switchbacks (right, left, right), which are separated by short connecting straights.

The road now sits at the base of an imposing hillside. Veering sharp left, there follows a long steady climb up the face of the hill, broken by a gentle Z-bend midway up the straight. Crash barriers provide protection on the coast side. At the end of the straight, there is a switchback to the right, which is followed by another long straight stretch of road. Towards the end of this, the road curves gently to the left. Now at the mid-point of the climb, views begin to open up ahead to the final set of switchbacks approaching the summit. Momentarily, the road levels off before a bridge.

Bending right to cross this, the gradient picks up gently and then more steeply along another long straight stretch of road to reach the foot of a sharp switchback to the left. After a shorter straight comes a marked bend to the right and then another bend to the left before the road heads up to the gate at the edge of the parking area.

Cycle left of the gate to avoid having to dismount. Beyond the parking bays, road quality improves on the gentle climb to the high point of the road on The Gap. Beyond the cattle grid, the summit is reached at the radio transmitter gate on the right.

DISTANCE 1.4 MILES
TOTAL HEIGHT GAIN 981 FEET
AVERAGE GRADIENT 13.6%
CLIMB PROFILE

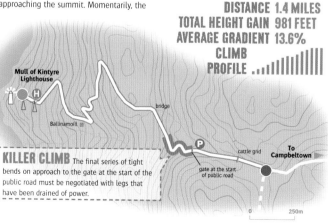

Mull of Kintyre Lighthouse

Ballinamoill

bridge

P

cattle grid

To Campbeltown

gate at the start of public road

KILLER CLIMB The final series of tight bends on approach to the gate at the start of the public road must be negotiated with legs that have been drained of power.

0   250m

KNAPDALE LOCH CAOLISPORT

Distance 2.6 miles/4.2km
Total Height Gain 594 ft/181m
Altitude Range 108-659ft/33-201m
Average Gradient 4.3%
Start Road junction, B8024/unclassified (NR 782772)
End Parking place above northeast end of Loch Arail (NR 814797)
Map OS Landranger 62
Rail Oban (46 miles)

A quiet hill road across the Kintyre peninsula affording picturesque snapshots of the sea lochs on either side of Kintyre.

Starting at the junction at Achahoish, the single-track road climbs gently to immediately sweep past the works area and nursery at Achahoish farm on the right.

Beyond a second crash barrier, as the road passes over a burn, the gradient steepens and continues at this pitch into the forest as it leaves behind the last house of Achahoish. As with the rest of the climb, there is good forward vision and ample passing places to assist overtaking. The road leads through a pleasant stretch of deciduous woodland, hiding the plantation forest which lies a short distance beyond.

Recent improvements are clearly evident for the next short stretch of road. To the right, the land falls steeply away beyond the forest to a small river valley below. The road continues to climb steadily, leaving behind the roadside border of deciduous woodland. A large roadside cutting to the left with a crash barrier to the right marks the end of the section of improved road.

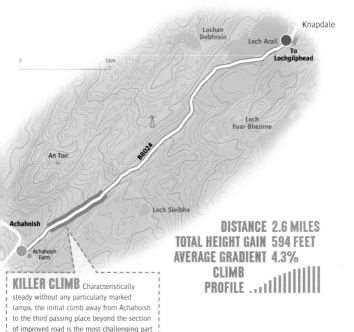

Knapdale

0   1km

An Torr

B8024

Loch Arail

To
Lochgilphead

Lochan
Dobhrain

Loch
Fuar-Bheinne

Loch Sleibhe

Achahoish

Achahoish
Farm

DISTANCE 2.6 MILES
TOTAL HEIGHT GAIN 594 FEET
AVERAGE GRADIENT 4.3%
CLIMB
PROFILE

KILLER CLIMB Characteristically
steady without any particularly marked
ramps, the initial climb away from Achahoish
to the third passing place beyond the section
of improved road is the most challenging part
of this route.

Road quality remains good for a country
road, although the surface is now less
smooth. Plantation forest to the right is set
back from the road with only a scattering of
trees on the rough open land around the
river banking, allowing views to open up
towards the hills above Loch Caolisport. The
climb continues steadily, albeit less
markedly than before.

Although plantation forest returns to the
left-hand side, there's no sense of being
hemmed in as the road passes through a
wide firebreak in the forest.

After a more marked sweep to the left
(starting at a crash barrier), then right, the
road changes direction on approach to the
summit above Loch Arail. The landscape
closes in for a few hundred yards with
steep banking on the open hillside to the
left and the narrowing of the firebreak in
the plantation to the right. However, on
bending right to reach the southeast side of
Loch Arail, views open up across the water.
The road continues to climb the hillside
above (very gently after traversing a small
knoll) to reach the summit at the large
parking place beyond the northeast side of
the loch.

KYLES OF BUTE TIGHNABRUAICH

Distance 3.67 miles/5.9km
Total Height Gain 581ft/177m
Altitude Range 10-591ft/3-180m
Average Gradient 3%
Start Road junction, A8003/B8000 (NR 975723)
End High point in roadside cutting (NR 992746)
Map OS Landranger 62
Rail Dunoon ferry terminal (23 miles), Gourock (44 miles)

A difficult start to this climb gives way to a changeable gradient as the road rises and falls unpredictably through the forest. The reward is panoramic views of the Kyles of Bute through occasional gaps in the forest cover on the slopes above Loch Riddon.

The climb away from Tighnabruaich starts on an unmarked road that branches off the shore road just before the Royal Bank of Scotland. Following a short straight, the narrow twin-track road kinks left, then more markedly right, after which the gradient stiffens and continues to steepen until the A8003 at the top of the hill is gained.

Turn right to join the A8003 and enjoy the respite that comes with a gentle climb on an improved single-track road. After a short distance, the road veers left and returns to twin-track as the national speed limit sign indicates that the village of Tighnabruaich has been left behind. Views are initially obscured by trees on either side as the road rises steadily away from the village. Beyond a passing place to the right, the road swings left and then right, with views opening up down to the lochside on the right. At this point, there is a long roadside parking place which has clearly been planned with the

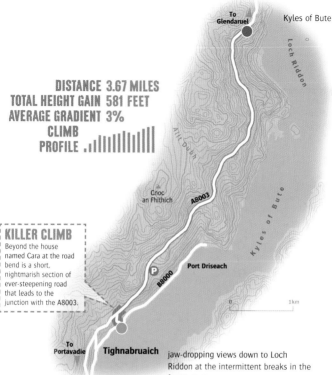

DISTANCE 3.67 MILES
TOTAL HEIGHT GAIN 581 FEET
AVERAGE GRADIENT 3%
CLIMB PROFILE

KILLER CLIMB

Beyond the house named Cara at the road bend is a short, nightmarish section of ever-steepening road that leads to the junction with the A8003.

Kyles of Bute

To Glendaruel

Loch Riddon

Allt Dubh

Cnoc an Fhithich

A8003

Kyles of Bute

Port Driseach

B8000

0   1km

To Portavadie

Tighnabruaich

photographer in mind. The initial ascent tops off when the road returns to single track soon after.

Having completed just over one quarter of the route's distance but gained almost one half of its height, what follows is now less of a distinctive road climb, as the ascent is interspersed with a series of downhills and flats. Nevertheless, continuing further along the wide twin-track A8003 makes for a pleasant and challenging road climb with jaw-dropping views down to Loch Riddon at the intermittent breaks in the forest cover.

The remainder of the climb involves a drop of 75 feet, followed by a climb of almost 175 feet to a secondary summit, a further drop of 100 feet and a final climb of more than 200 feet. However, flats and gradient changes make this much less straightforward and it does not comprise four distinct stages in profile. The climb finally tops out inside a road cutting before descending more markedly down to and beyond the large NTS viewpoint.

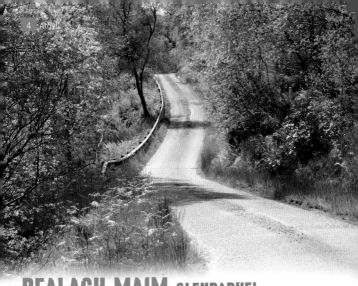

BEALACH MAIM GLENDARUEL

Distance 2.2 miles/3.5km
Total Height Gain 1063ft/324m
Altitude Range 20-1050 feet/6-320m
Average Gradient 9.4%
Start Road bend (NR 995830)
End High point between distinctive tree and fencepost (NR 973832)
Map OS Landranger 55
Rail Dunoon ferry terminal (23 miles), Gourock (44 miles), Arrochar and Tarbet (35 miles)

A taxing climb on a quiet hill road through plantation forest at an average gradient of almost 10% over two miles.

The ascent starts uneventfully enough on the valley bottom, with good views from the outset. The gradient becomes more marked, particularly when the road passes a ruined farmshed and bears left. The road then veers to the right in stages, as it climbs steadily and steeply across the hillside. Tree-lined on the upslope, good views are afforded to the right across the valley floor.

At the end of the straight, a tight left switchback reverses the direction of travel and takes the road into the forest. The gradient lessens momentarily, before returning to a very steep climb where a crash barrier starts on the left. Travelling southwest, this section comprises a series of short and steep climbs, interspersed with shorter flat steps. The road is generally straight, affording good forward vision; tree-felling has also opened up views down to

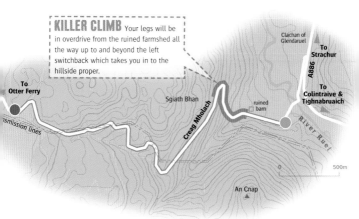

KILLER CLIMB Your legs will be in overdrive from the ruined farmshed all the way up to and beyond the left switchback which takes you in to the hillside proper.

Clachan of Glendaruel
To Strachur
A886

To Otter Ferry

Sgiath Bhan

Creag Mholach

ruined barn

To Colintraive & Tighnabruaich

River Ruel

Transmission lines

0   500m

An Cnap ▲

DISTANCE 2.2 MILES
TOTAL HEIGHT GAIN 1063 FEET
AVERAGE GRADIENT 9.4%
CLIMB PROFILE ▁▁▁▂▃▄▅▆▇█

the left. The quality is also good, although the centre of the road is rough with vegetative growth. On passing under overhead pylons, there is a slight dip.

Beyond this, a sweeping change of direction to the right marks a return to steeper hill climbing and an improvement in road quality, with a broad border of heather and ferns to the left. After a short tough section of ascent, the road veers left as it passes once again under pylons and rougher grassland replaces the plantation forest to the right. Sweeping bends to the right follow before the road changes direction once more to bear west, shadowing the route of the pylons.

Tight bends are soon succeeded by a longer straight, steepening where plantation forest returns to the roadside on the left. As the forest peels away and the road passes under the pylons for the last time, there is much more open aspect and a levelling of the gradient which continues up to a fencepost. This is a lower summit, beyond which the road sweeps gently to the right and more markedly to the left. Following the line of the trees on the right, the road rises up for a final climb to reach the true summit at a vague point between a distinctive tree and fencepost.

Perthshire has earned a reputation as the hub of cycling in the Highlands, if not the whole of Scotland, in recent years. Most notably, Etape Caledonia, Britain's first closed road cycle event, brings more than 5000 cyclists to the county every May, offering a King of the Mountains challenge on the slopes of Schiehallion, just after the halfway point. The Etape is the lynchpin of the Highland Perthshire Cycling Festival, which is aimed at promoting the local cycling operators, events and bike-friendly facilities that cater for two-wheelers of all abilities and disciplines year round.

Surprisingly, despite being home to some of the best hillclimbs in Highland Scotland, this aspect of Perthshire's cycling feast of treasures is undersold. There are, in fact, many times more classic Perthshire climbs than can be described in the following pages, but those that won out offer fantastic range for the hillclimber, including the short but vicious pair of climbs above Glen Garry, the steady grind up to Loch na Craige from Aberfeldy, the ascent of the wild moorland on the southern flanks of Ben Lawers and the excruciating first half-mile to be endured by those who tackle the route from Kenmore to the road summit of A'Chrois.

PITLOCHRY AND WESTERN PERTHSHIRE

BEN LAWERS MILTON MORENISH, LOCH TAY

Distance 4.2 miles/6.7km
Total Height Gain 1296ft/395m
Altitude Range 476-1762ft/145-537m
Average Gradient 5.9%
Start Road end/track junction
(NN 616358)
End Road/track junction (NN 602394)
Map OS Landranger 51
Rail Crianlarich Station (18 miles),
Pitlochry Station (33 miles)

A long climb up to the Lochan na Lairige on a well conditioned single-track road, which combines brutal and gentle inclines as it passes through a range of Perthshire landscapes.

Those with sadomasochistic tendencies should seek out the road end at Milton Morenish where you can expect to endure a crippling climb from a standing start on a badly rutted straight. The gradient eases back at the end of this, but continues to challenge through left and right bends, topping out on reaching the A827. Turn right for a transitional section of gentle climbing and flats leading to the alternative start point at the road for Ben Lawers and the Bridge of Balgie.

Turning left, you're faced with a severe climb, soon sweeping around a left-hand bend and bearing left at the road junction. It's a challenging climb through plantation forest, with the taxing gradient persisting through a forest break, a sweeping right-hand bend and a straight beyond. Finally, on reaching an opening, the gradient eases.

Respite does not last long, as a return to steeper climbing comes on approach to a right-hand bend as you re-enter forest. What follows is a series of straights

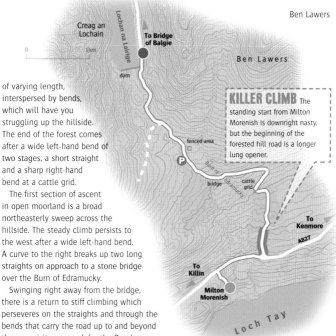

KILLER CLIMB The standing start from Milton Morenish is downright nasty, but the beginning of the forested hill road is a longer lung opener.

of varying length, interspersed by bends, which will have you struggling up the hillside. The end of the forest comes after a wide left-hand bend of two stages, a short straight and a sharp right-hand bend at a cattle grid.

The first section of ascent in open moorland is a broad northeasterly sweep across the hillside. The steady climb persists to the west after a wide left-hand bend. A curve to the right breaks up two long straights on approach to a stone bridge over the Burn of Edramucky.

Swinging right away from the bridge, there is a return to stiff climbing which perseveres on the straights and through the bends that carry the road up to and beyond the new visitor car park for the Ben Lawers Nature Reserve. Eventually, the climb eases back at the site of the old visitor centre, now fenced off.

A more gradual ascent before the final push carries the road around four wide bends, passing a track junction to the left. The right-hand bend beyond this point is followed by a straight, aiming for the crag face of Creag an Lochain.

A further right-hand bend brings the dam into full view and the thigh-burn begins for a final time. Two straights, short then long, are broken up by a left-hand bend as the road climbs to a cutting through a rocky

outcrop. A final steep ramp carries the road up to a high point above the dam to reach the track that heads down to Lochan na Lairige. From here, an undulating pedal for 1.5 miles above the loch only gains a further 12m in height.

DISTANCE 4.2 MILES
TOTAL HEIGHT GAIN 1296 FEET
AVERAGE GRADIENT 5.9%
CLIMB PROFILE

A'CHROIS KENMORE

Distance 3.25 miles/5.2km
Total Height Gain 1375ft/419m
Altitude Range 364-1736ft/111-529m
Average Gradient 8%
Start Road junction, minor/A827
(NN 775451)
End Road bend (NN 804422)
Map OS Landranger 52
Rail Crianlarich Station (30 miles),
Pitlochry Station (21 miles)

Not a climb to be underestimated, especially as it presents a further mile of contour-crunching ascent in the mid-section after an intensely brutal climb away from Kenmore.

Start at the road junction just off the A827 on the edge of Kenmore. Cyclists might be better advised if the roadsign at the foot of this climb warning of a weak bridge ahead, was switched to 'weak legs ahead'. The start is unforgiving and the pain does not relent until many metres in height have been gained over not so many metres in distance.

The first of four switchbacks on the lower slopes is reached by way of three short straights, separated by gentle bends. The second switchback, this time to the right, follows more quickly after two short straights. A longer straight awaits, and although there is an easing midway, the early and latter parts are brutal, before ending at a third switchback, this time to the left. There then follows a series of straights of varying lengths and trajectories as the roads clambers its way up the forested slopes of the valley side with little respite to be found – all its variations are tough. Eventually, a fourth switchback, again to the left and with a very steep inside bend, carries the road around to the foot of a long straight. There's light at the

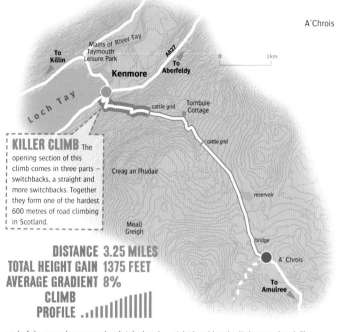

KILLER CLIMB The opening section of this climb comes in three parts – switchbacks, a straight and more switchbacks. Together they form one of the hardest 600 metres of road climbing in Scotland.

DISTANCE 3.25 MILES
TOTAL HEIGHT GAIN 1375 FEET
AVERAGE GRADIENT 8%
CLIMB PROFILE ..ıı‖‖‖‖‖

end of the tunnel as a couple of right-hand bends take you beyond the forest and the gradient finally eases after crossing a cattle grid to emerge into open countryside.

A transitional section of gentle climbing, hillside traversing and gradual descent follows as the road cuts across farmland to reach and then traverse the bridge in front of the picturesque Tombuie Cottage.

From here, the climbing starts all over again. Move steeply away from the cottage, following a couple of short straights, divided by a right-hand bend to re-enter forest. At the second left-hand bend at the end of the second short straight, the road emerges steeply from the forest, aiming for a sharp

right-hand bend a little way ahead. The landscape is now more upland, and rougher grasses border the road. A longer straight rises steeply up to a left-hand bend, after which an even longer straight awaits. This aims directly up the hillside, picking up plantation forest for company and shelter on the left. A right-hand bend is taken to leave the forest behind.

Climbing is now much less severe and the route ahead less straightforward as it undulates and rises gently. It passes a lochan with a small building, a stone bridge, and a sharp left-hand bend to summit on the bleak moorland at the track junction marked by a steel gate on your right.

LOCH NA CRAIGE ABERFELDY

Distance 3.7 miles/6km
Total Height Gain 1014ft/309m
Altitude Range 295-1309ft/90-399m
Average Gradient 5.2%
Start Crossroads at Aberfeldy putting green (NN 852493)
End Road bend (NN 882460)
Map OS Landranger 52
Rail Pitlochry Station (15 miles)

Although there are a few steep pitches, this is one of the less taxing ways to accumulate 1000ft of net height gain in Highland Scotland.

Climb gently away from the crossroads of Taybridge Drive/Terrace on the A826 and follow a right-hand bend to reach traffic lights at the junction with the A827. Continue ahead on a more uneven road surface, leaving the town behind after Urlar

Road. A swing to the right is followed by a sweeping left-hand bend to emerge abruptly at the traffic lights which regulate traffic flow over the Moness Burn.

After the bridge, the road banks to the right to start a steeper section of ascent and trees close in as it makes its way up to the entrance of the Moness Resort.

The road then veers left and open aspect returns on the upslope, the gradient easing as the road skirts the upper fringes of the country club. Beyond, a gentle Z-bend is followed by the first of two long straights that cut across and up the hillside. Initially closed in, after crossing the burn forest cover peters out on the downslope and views open up over Aberfeldy, the Tay Valley and the hills beyond. There is a further softening of the gradient at the right-hand bend beyond the second straight.

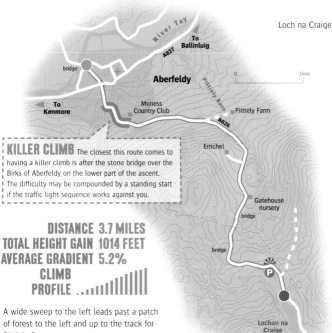

Loch na Craige

River Tay

A827

To Ballinluig

bridge

Aberfeldy

0   1km

To Kenmore

Moness Country Club

Pittiely Burn

Pittiely Farm

A826

Errichel

Gatehouse nursery

bridge

bridge

P

Lochan na Craige

KILLER CLIMB The closest this route comes to having a killer climb is after the stone bridge over the Birks of Aberfeldy on the lower part of the ascent. The difficulty may be compounded by a standing start if the traffic light sequence works against you.

DISTANCE 3.7 MILES
TOTAL HEIGHT GAIN 1014 FEET
AVERAGE GRADIENT 5.2%
CLIMB
PROFILE ....

A wide sweep to the left leads past a patch of forest to the left and up to the track for Pittiely Farm.

From here, steeper climbing resumes. The initial pitch up to a right-hand bend gets the blood pumping, and the steady climb beyond maintains this heart rate. The road becomes hemmed in between steeply sloping forest and the wooded valley of the Pittiely Burn, steepening on approach to a sharper right-hand bend, before easing back on the straight beyond.

After the track to Errichel, there's a more open aspect again. A sweeping left-hand bend leads to a short straight on approach to the lofty Gatehouse Nursery, and the gradient eases. The road sweeps past the nursery with a right-hand bend and the

incline picks up again.

Passing through a gap in a stone wall, the road enters plantation forest – in summer you're likely to acquire a battalion of midges for company. A narrow stone bridge is soon passed, able to carry just one vehicle at a time. After passing another stone bridge, the road banks sharply to the left, a sweep to the right later taking the road up to the viewpoint car park entrance. Continue ahead, easing back to reach the summit just beyond the left hand-bend, where a track junction joins the road on the right.

101

GLEN GARRY DUO NEAR KILLIECRANKIE

Distance South: 0.65 miles/1km.
North: 0.75 miles/1.2km
Total Height Gain South: 351ft/107m.
North: 367ft/112m
Altitude Range South: 410-761ft/125-232m. North: 387-755ft/118-230m
Average Gradient South: 10.2%. North: 9.3%
Start South: Road junction, minor/B8019 (NN 913609).
North: Passing place (NN 909628)
End South: Fonvuick entrance (NN 913609).
North: Road bend (NN 913618)
Map OS Landranger 43
Rail Pitlochry Station (3 miles)

You're spoilt for choice with these short but formidable climbs up to Tenandry above the Pass of Killiecrankie, each at an average gradient of around 10%.
South (From Garry Bridge): Immediately after the Garry Bridge car park, turn off the B8019 in the direction of Tenandry.

Climbing steeply from the outset on a narrow road, the lower half of this climb winds its way up through mature forest. The gradient changes frequently, but it never eases back to provide sufficient respite from the exertions and never ramps up so dramatically to require road wobble. Towards the mid-point of the climb, the road emerges from the forest on a straighter and stiffer section to approach and then pass a church in the hamlet of Tenandry. Beyond, a sweeping bend to the right leaves behind the last few houses for the final climb. Although a line of roadside trees obscures vision slightly, the downslope is now farmland and views open up to the Pass of Killiecrankie and across to Ben Vrackie and the Beinn a'Ghlo mountain complex. Continue to rise steeply, taking left-hand bends which cut around the hillside to gain the summit marked by two trees sitting on a small knoll next

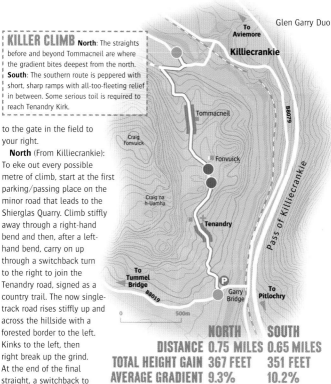

Glen Garry Duo

KILLER CLIMB **North**: The straights before and beyond Tommacneil are where the gradient bites deepest from the north.
South: The southern route is peppered with short, sharp ramps with all-too-fleeting relief in between. Some serious toil is required to reach Tenandry Kirk.

to the gate in the field to your right.

North (From Killiecrankie): To eke out every possible metre of climb, start at the first parking/passing place on the minor road that leads to the Shierglas Quarry. Climb stiffly away through a right-hand bend and then, after a left-hand bend, carry on up through a switchback turn to the right to join the Tenandry road, signed as a country trail. The now single-track road rises stiffly up and across the hillside with a forested border to the left. Kinks to the left, then right break up the grind. At the end of the final straight, a switchback to the left reverses the direction of travel and, soon after, the gradient eases back. The incline is now more gentle as the road winds around the forest edge. A more marked left-hand bend is soon followed by a return to stiffer climbing for a short pitch, easing back to coincide with the departure from the forest to the left. Soon after, the road rears up for its steepest pitch yet, which leads up to and beyond the steading of Tommacneil. After

an S-bend, the gradient starts to slacken in stages and a series of shorter straights bring the road up to a sweeping bend to the left. The climbing pares back to allow for a gentle pedal up to the summit that lies at the right-hand bend just after the track leading to Fonvuick.

	NORTH	**SOUTH**
DISTANCE	0.75 MILES	0.65 MILES
TOTAL HEIGHT GAIN	367 FEET	351 FEET
AVERAGE GRADIENT	9.3%	10.2%
CLIMB PROFILE		

STAT PAGE

PAGE		DISTANCE (MILES)	ASCENT (FEET)	GRADIENT
86	Mull of Kintyre	1.4	981	13.6
38	Achtuie	1	702	13.6
80	Bealach Feith nan Laogh	1.6	1027	11.9
102	Glen Garry, South	0.65	351	10.2
24	Cairn o' Mount	2.1	1068	9.6
44	Berriedale Braes, South	0.9	446	9.6
92	Bealach Maim	2.2	1063	9.4
102	Glen Garry, North	0.75	367	9.3
56	Bealach na Gaoithe	1.6	781	9.1
76	Lundavra Road	1	469	8.9
72	Castlebay, Isle of Barra	0.7	321	8.7
30	The Lecht	1.9	883	8.6
70	Loch Beag, Reinigeadal	1.2	525	8.6
18	Craigowl Hill	2.4	1043	8.3
62	Bealach Ratagan	2.6	1099	8.2
82	Glen Leidle	1.5	659	8.1
98	A'Chrois	3.25	1375	8.0
66	Calum's Road, North	0.9	358	7.7
40	Heights of Dochcarty	1.9	748	7.6
60	Bealach na Ba, Loch Kishorn	5.25	2028	7.3
28	Hill of Findon	1.33	512	7.3
48	Saxa Vord	2.3	896	7.2
44	Berriedale Braes, North	1.4	541	7.2
16	Dundee Law	1.4	525	7.2
58	Bealach na Ba, Applecross	5.5	2014	6.9
66	Calum's Road, South	0.55	190	6.6
68	Quiraing	2.5	794	6.1
96	Ben Lawers	4.2	1296	5.9
14	Pole Hill	2.4	728	5.8
54	Badrallach Heights	2.2	679	5.8
20	Caterthuns	2.1	614	5.6
26	Brimmond Hill	2.2	630	5.5
36	Carn an t-Suidhe	5	1388	5.3
100	Loch na Craige	3.7	1014	5.2
34	Cairn Gorm Ski Road	3.67	994	5.1
46	Wideford Hill	3	774	4.9
50	Quinag	3.5	797	4.3
88	Knapdale	2.6	594	4.3
90	Kyles of Bute	3.67	581	3.0
78	Glen Coe to Rannoch Moor	15.1	1378	1.7